CONJOINT MARITAL THERAPY

R.V. Fitzgerald

CONJOINT MARITAL THERAPY

Jason Aronson

Publishers

Contents

Introduction

*A*MORE COMPLETE and accurate title for this book would be "One Therapist's Understanding and Method of Conducting Conjoint Marital Psychotherapy." This expanded title—although admittedly too awkward to use—nevertheless conveys my recognition that there are a number of styles of conducting such therapy.

This book can be understood by an intelligent person who has had no training or experience in any branch of the helping professions. However, it is being written primarily for both beginning and more experienced therapists, whatever their discipline—medicine, psychiatry, psychology, social work, counseling, or the ministry. To derive *maximum returns* from this book, therapists should at least be familiar with the fundamentals of psychological development and developmental levels, psychoanalysis, classical Freudian as well as neo-Freudian ego psychology, small-group dynamics, communicational processes, interviewing techniques, and psychotherapy. From supervising others—mainly social workers and psychologists—in marital therapy, it is my impression that it is easier to move to conjoint marital therapy from group therapy than from individual therapy.

I cannot identify in advance the particular patient population for whom this therapy would be more effective than alternative forms of therapy, except that they must be in a viable marriage relationship. Based on my experience, I think that any patient who is a "good candidate" for psychotherapy in general is also a good candidate for conjoint marital psychotherapy. In my thirteen-years work with this type of therapy, treatment has turned out to be brief, averaging six months for those who become genuinely involved. In my previous fourteen years of experience with individual, mainly psychoanalytically oriented, psychotherapy, treatment tended to be of considerably longer duration. My own transition to conjoint marital therapy was not an easy one. To my surprise, certain couples (usually young and married not more than two to five years), were satisfied and improved, markedly to moderately, after only four to six weekly sessions. It was rarer to come upon those who continued treatment longer than two years. As a result, my patient turnover increased and my waiting list disappeared, only to reappear once again after this form of therapy had gained credibility and respectability among patients and referral sources.

Premises

4   It is generally admitted that those who are intimate and

seek basic need gratification from each other have a great impact on each other. Such impact varies in closeness, intensity, duration, complexity, and meaningfulness; it could be thought of in terms of different kinds and degrees of relationship, as, for instance, clerk–customer or employer–employee. Here I am concerned with that complex, often long-lasting, terribly meaningful, close/distant relationship of marriage. In treating couples, symptoms and character traits can be directly observed, and some kind of intervention is promptly possible. The patients' level of emotional participation is maximized, since the treatment takes place within the emotionally charged atmosphere of a real, ongoing, vitally important relationship; all these factors intensify the therapeutic process.

Any sort of meaningful change in one spouse must result in a corresponding change in the other. It is better that these adjustments be made simultaneously; if they take place only in sequence, the change in the second partner has to occur promptly, so that the first change is not vitiated. For example, a wife is in therapy for disabling headaches. What happens to her husband once she begins to assert herself directly, rather than through her symptomatic behavior? Perhaps the husband distorts and exaggerates even her quite appropriate assertiveness by experiencing it as biting criticism. In a sense, the situation becomes political, that is, a question of relative power between the patient–therapist alliance and the husband–patient relationship. Will the therapist have enough power to "cure" his patient of her headaches? Or will the husband crush the tender plant that the patient and the therapist, working together within the therapist's sphere of influence, have nurtured. When the husband is present and a patient, however, and when the marriage is considered still another patient, that particular problem of power is avoided. The husband may be able to learn the what, the how, and the

5

why of his reaction to his wife's new assertiveness.

Value Judgments

We must become aware of our value judgments as to marriage and divorce. It is safe to assume that we start out with a positive attitude toward marriage and its maintenance and a preference for avoiding divorce, if possible. We generally believe in the family as the proper place for children to be nurtured. In the headache situation above, let us assume that the therapist and the patient have enough power to sustain the wife's assertiveness. Her self-esteem improves markedly; she becomes more self-confident and less dependent upon her husband's approval and support. One might conclude that the therapy is going along at a great rate! But what's happening at home? Since the husband is reacting with ever-increasing resentment to these changes in his wife (sometimes she may even feel free enough to get a little nasty), he reaches the point where he can no longer stand her—and gets a divorce. For the patient, this result of treatment is partly good and partly bad; the next husband *she* selects will probably be quite different from her former one. For the children and the husband, however, I consider the result totally unsatisfactory. We can predict that the former husband will select another wife, when he does, with the same or similar personality as his first wife. Couples able to work out these neurotic conflicts usually remain together on a better adaptational level. Successful treatment of marital pathology diagnosed early should improve the family atmosphere and avoid or minimize later development of psychological disturbances in the couple's children.

Another clinical example of the hazards of successful treatment of a married patient involves a woman who entered

6

therapy for treatment of agoraphobia of such serious proportions that her fear of being alone in the streets had rendered her virtually housebound. Indeed, her husband had to leave his responsible executive position to bring her to my office during the early months of her therapy. In her individual therapy the wife reported no complaints or protests on the part of her husband, in spite of the considerable inconvenience her dependency created for him. His generosity and acceptance of the situation seemed boundless. The patient was unable to throw any light on his unusual acquiescence. As my patient progressed in therapy and her phobia improved, she began to report inexplicable irritability and apprehensiveness in her husband. He would worry when the patient attempted to go shopping alone and would call home and check to see how she had made out on her own. As she took more risks, her husband's agitation increased, and he began to make negative predictions about what might happen. He began to drink more, but not to any serious proportion. I took a quite insouciant attitude toward the husband. Since I was working more or less within a psychoanalytic frame and applying its strictures rigidly, I could not have seen him. The wife did not indicate he was receptive to therapy, and I did not suggest that he seek treatment with another therapist. It was obvious to me that the husband's aversive reactions were slowing the wife's progress; I felt him to be our enemy. Fortunately, the husband made the necessary inner adjustments to his wife's newly found independence on his own, and this treatment ended successfully without any long-term rupture in their relationship. I now feel that I contributed to the husband's pain by allowing him to struggle alone with his conflicts and anxieties about the therapy-induced changes in his wife.

My experience with conjoint marital psychotherapy has helped me understand the dynamics of those husbands who positively encourage their wives to become or remain phobic. While the wife entertains an adulterous fantasy, in some instances the husband experiences a fantasy of his wife's having an affair. The two fantasies dovetail, and the wife's phobia protects them *both* from this anticipated disaster. The husband's fantasy may arise out of low self-esteem, projection of his unacceptable wishes onto her, or memories of his mother's adulterous behavior. His anxieties obviously deserve as much attention as those of his ostensibly "sicker" wife. Again conjoint psychotherapy is one way of reaching this goal.

I shall only summarize another example briefly. An attractive young woman tolerated, with minimal protest, an unconsummated marriage and a female-underclothing fetish in her husband for three years before he sought therapy. The husband and I need her help if he is to become a more effective male with her. And we are not likely to get it until we understand her need to go along with his behavior. Inner resistances to change are difficult enough to deal with in any form of therapy; it is perilous to neglect outer reinforcement of them.

Transference—Countertransference

Spouses are, without a doubt, valuable sources of information about each other, both in obtaining an accurate and complete history and in discovering the nature of their relationship. Because the patient may react to me so differently from the way he or she interacts with the spouse, I may be unable to develop any clear, undistorted idea about what their relationship is actually like. Consequently, transference–countertransference data are not necessarily accurate but may be frequently confusing and massively inaccurate.

How could this nice, tractable, cooperative patient, who is

making such beautiful progress with me, ever be a "bitch on wheels" at home with "that bastard"? The danger of over-identification with the patient is obvious; and I am suggesting that conjoint marital therapy is *one* way of minimizing our chances of falling into such a trap. Certain pieces of information that the patient may not be able to tell you may be of vital importance. One woman, for example, had seen several psychiatrists and been treated for her "depression" in several different ways. None of the previous therapists, however, ever learned that she was a child batterer. With the couple in conjoint marital therapy, this information emerged in the sixth interview. When I was puzzled by the wife's profound agitation, the husband quietly said, "Maybe we had better tell him what happened." Here, at least, we had the opportunity to understand and to work out therapeutically the husband's role in the pathology. He could be a domineering slave-driver; the abuse the child gets from the mother could really be meant for the husband. (I am, of course, fully aware of the oversimplification here.) In this particular example, the wife was completely unable to function as a mother, and the husband could not learn how to help her act in this capacity. Indeed, I had the impression, which I did not stop to interpret, that the husband needed to get rid of her and to function as both mother and father in order to satisfy some needs and hostilities within himself. In this case I regarded the relatively friendly divorce, with the husband awarded custody of the children, as the best possible solution.

Identification with the Therapist

Often later—but sometimes even early—in therapy, when the therapeutic focus is on one spouse, the other, by identification with the therapist's different attitudes and manner, 9 comes to act as an auxiliary therapist. This can occur both in and between sessions. For example, if one spouse attacks the therapist in a sarcastic or insulting manner for something he has said or done, the therapist may pick out what is reasonable in the tirade and own up to his mistake or his failure at having made himself clear. After the patient has calmed down, the therapist can then focus on the negative-transference aspects of the outburst, if he does not already know where they came from. Meanwhile, the other spouse is listening and learning; at times the therapist may have to block him out and insist that he remain in an observer role. From this the listening spouse may learn two separate, but intimately related, lessons: (a) a different and more successful way of dealing with his angry, or frightened, or hostile–clinging (or whatever) spouse; and (b) what inadvertently triggered memories related to bad experiences with important figures out of the spouse's past, which may pave the way for some understanding of and empathy for the spouse.

It should be clear that what is being dramatized here, and interpreted as quickly as tact and closeness to consciousness permit, are transference reactions, especially negative ones. Since the couple are more heavily transferred, one to the other, and the presence of the two of them dilutes the transference to the therapist, these reactions occur much more frequently between them when the therapist is in the observer–interpreter role. When the treatment is successful, transferences are analyzed out, or at least modified, so that one spouse experiences the other as the real person he is, rather than through existing transference images. Their reality-testing with each other is thus reexamined and its accuracy enhanced. It is true that the spouses may distort and even make use of the comments made by the therapist as clubs with which to beat each other. This must be dealt with either on the spot or later. I may have said that a husband seemed to be reacting to his wife *as if* he were experiencing her to be like his mother. At some point during or between sessions the wife may then say accusingly, "Stop treating me like your mother; I'm not your mother." Or I may have explained to a wife that *according to her own* view she seemed to be feeling guilty about what she regarded as "bad" thoughts or feelings. Distorting this, the husband may throw the blaming statement in her face: "Dr. Fitzgerald said it was bad for you to have such thoughts!" It then becomes necessary to clarify what I meant, usually by saying something like, "Apparently I didn't make myself clear enough last week. Let me try again." I then repeat the interpretation in other words, perhaps in two or three different ways, and then attempt to explore the need of the one spouse to blame, accuse, or arouse guilt in the other. This can be done immediately or when the opportunity arises during the interview.

Diminished Patient Dependency on Therapist

Since patient–therapist transferences are diluted and, in some measure, many patients take over a therapeutic function with each other, undue and prolonged patient dependency on the therapist is avoided. This has been documented, in my experience, by the significantly shorter duration of conjoint marital therapy than of individual psychotherapy, no matter what the clinical condition or diagnostic label of the identified patient.

At the end of this book, I have supplied an extensive reading list, including most of the written sources of my knowledge about personality theory, diagnosis, and psychotherapy in general. This list is an attempt to express my gratitude to my teachers, many of whom I have never 11 met in person. I hope, also, that it will stimulate the reader to turn to these books and articles, which, because of their usefulness to me, have become my favorites.

I am indebted to those of my patients who have given me the opportunity to learn from them. They have helped me to find what was meaningful and useful to them. I am deeply indebted also to many of my teachers at the Menninger Foundation School of Psychiatry; to my analyst George A. Richardson, M.D., who helped me to learn about myself; to my supervisors David Leach, M.D., and Andrew S. Watson, M.D., who helped me to use myself in treating others, the former in individual psychotherapy, the latter in conjoint marital psychotherapy. When Dr. Jason Aronson accepted my manuscript contingent on my expanding it to include many more clinical examples, I accepted this challenge ambivalently. While I was in the process of revision, I came to hate him and the book. Now, with the whole manuscript before me, I can appreciate the wisdom of his editorial judgment. I also appreciate the excellent editorial assistance of Joan Tapper Siegel of the Jason Aronson staff. I wish also to express my appreciation to Hella Freud Bernays for her excellent editorial assistance.

Last, but far from least, I am grateful to my wife Margaret, social worker and skilled therapist. She has taught me much about loving (she's good at this), much about marriage (she's very good at this), much about fighting (she's definitely skillful at this). She has been my best friend and, when I have consulted her about my work, has appeared admirably in the role of severest critic.

It must be clear by now that I have taken ideas and techniques from many places. I really cannot identify with precision where or from whom I obtained what I have made my own. In any event, I alone take full responsibility for what is in this book.

CHAPTER I

The Patients

Problems Presented

W HEN THERE are spouses in an ongoing, meaningful, viable marital relationship, with both patients receptive to participation in therapy, three differing sets of circumstances may exist at the time of the initial contact (usually made by telephone) with a therapist who restricts his practice to outpatient psychotherapy:

1. The problem may be identified as marital by one or both spouses.
2. The problem may be concerned with an offspring —child or adolescent.
3. The problem may be some form of psychopathology in one or both.

I have been doing conjoint marital psychotherapy for thirteen years and have had the experience of working with over 250 couples who have become meaningfully involved in the therapy; most patients who call upon me are aware of the way I work and come to me seeking this specific form of therapy. Their referral source—whether that source was another professional or a current or former patient—has acquainted them with this particular approach. The couple have evidently been sufficiently impressed to seek therapy. It surprises me that even patients whose treatment I considered unsuccessful or who terminated therapy with negative feelings have later referred others to me. Therefore, I do not have to take the initiative as often as I formerly had to in structuring the therapy.

Where the problem is marital, conjoint marital psychotherapy is usually accepted readily. It is only a little more difficult to structure the therapy for patients with the other two types of problems so that they become involved. There are, of course, exceptions, which occur most commonly when the parents have already rigidly identified the problem as being within the child or the adolescent; they are unable to consider anything other than sending him off, like some broken home appliance, to a repair shop to be "fixed." Some patients may have to be eased into conjoint marital psychotherapy by having the whole family, or perhaps just the parents and the child or adolescent involved, seen together by the therapist to begin with. Some selection or combination of individual therapy, family group therapy, and/or conjoint marital psychotherapy then usually develops.

Patient Characteristics

14 Most of my patients are from the middle- or upper-income

groups and live in the suburbs or the more affluent sections of the city. Among my current patients, in about 20 percent of the couples, one spouse is a physician or a university professor. With the extension of psychiatric insurance coverage to those in the lower-income brackets, as, for example, in the United Automobile Workers' contracts, increasing numbers of patients from such groups are applying for treatment, but the number is still low, less than 1 percent. The employed spouses of the remaining couples are in many different occupations: salesmen, engineers, architects, corporation executives, self-employed small businessmen, accountants, etc. In one out of five couples, the wife is also employed, usually more by choice then from economic necessity.

My patients tend to cluster at two stages of the developmental cycle of marriage. Approximately 45 percent are in the early phase of the relationship, that is, married seven or eight years or less; they are in the twenty-five to thirty age group, and their children are early elementary school pupils or younger. As might be expected, the next cluster, about 40 percent, is at another critical time in life and in marriage; these couples have been married about fifteen to twenty years, are at the forty to fifty-five age level, and have at least one teen-ager. In this group, the crisis often revolves around the older teen-ager's struggle for autonomy and separation from the family unit, as well as around the problems and conflicts of middle age to be expected in the parents. Less than 2 percent of the remaining patients I have treated have been over sixty-five; accordingly, about 13 to 14 percent have been married between eight and fifteen years and are in the thirty-five to forty-five age range.

Of the 100 patients (fifty couples) on my current active list, 10 percent have been previously married; of these only two have been married more than once before.

Acceptance Terms

At the outset, I explicitly state that I accept patients for therapy only if the relationship is intact enough that the spouses can maintain themselves between sessions with some reasonable degree of control. Accordingly, few seriously disturbed people even apply for therapy with me. No patient is rejected, however, unless one spouse refuses to participate (I regard this as collusive) or he is unable to afford my standard fee. In certain circumstances I reduce the fee or arrange for a deferred-payment plan. Older teen-agers may be accepted for individual psychotherapy without the participation of their parents, but I insist upon one family diagnostic interview. In traditional diagnostic terms, less than 5 percent of my patients are overtly psychotic or borderline, about 10 percent have affective disorders, and the rest can be characterized as having neurotic or character disorders. About half of those in the two latter categories I consider in the moderately to seriously disturbed range.

The Third Patient, the Therapist

A few revelations concerning my personal history should give readers an insight into my orientation and style. I did not marry until after my psychoanalysis; my wife is a psychiatric social worker, trained and experienced in psychoanalytically oriented individual and group psychotherapist. Both of us are former Roman Catholics, mainly of Irish descent, although I had one German grandfather. We share value systems and a humanistic, agnostic, christian (and I would emphasize the small c) philosophical world view. A fertility problem deprived us of the opportunity for parenthood, and we lacked the courage to adopt children. This latter circumstance, I believe, made our work with patients and as teachers of other mental health professionals especially important and meaningful; we often talk and feel about our patients as another couple might talk and feel about their children.

Throughout my childhood and adolescence, my parents, my seven-years'-younger brother, and my sixteen-years'-younger sister and I lived with my mother's parents. This gave me the opportunity to observe and to experience at first hand two generations and two marriages, as well as the workings of an extended family system. Our family group had close contact with my matriarchal grandmother's clannish Irish family as well as peripheral contact with my maternal grandfather's German relatives. We had no direct contact with my father's family, since they lived across the continent on the West Coast. In my early days my parents' marriage seemed warm and close, but when I was about thirteen or fourteen it became quite conflicted, and when I was 25 they were divorced. At the time I felt myself thrust into the role of negotiator. I now realize that I had an inner need to assume that role. I also strongly felt the pull of conflicting loyalties, as well as my parents' pain in separating from each other. My father was in the army reserve, and he was called to active duty in early 1942; I was then nineteen. At that point, due to his emotional as well as geographical distance from the family, I became the effective head of the family. At least, that is how I felt and acted. By this time my grandmother was a near-total invalid, the result of a stroke she had had five years earlier. My grandfather devoted himself diligently to caring for her at home and, accordingly, had little interest and energy left for anything else. I lent whatever emotional support I could to the family group and felt almost paternal toward my younger brother and sister. I assumed this position, but I resented it far more than I realized at the time.

Having survived this ordeal bruised but relatively intact, 17 the potential marriage and family therapist was already lying there within me, awaiting only the appropriate time and opportunity to emerge, which arrived in 1961. In that year Andrew S. Watson, M.D., arrived in Toledo, where I was practicing, to give a seminar on conjoint marital psychotherapy. I was doing individual psychotherapy at the time and beginning to feel somewhat stale and ineffective; the timing for something new and different was precisely right for me. Within a month a couple came to me in need of and receptive to conjoint marital psychotherapy; I turned to Dr. Watson and received his help in learning this new approach.

A few words are in order about the difficulty I experienced in making the transition from one form of therapy to the other. Most individual psychotherapists who work within a psychoanalytic framework tend to be silent, to wait patiently, to pile up an abundance of evidence before making an intervention. They await the development of and attend closely to transference–countertransference phenomena. As a rule such professionals are sharply focused on intrapsychic content. The therapist with this orientation and experience is apt to think of "the patient" as having the disease process going on within him, although the former would not, of course, totally neglect interpersonal processes nor the impact of the multitudinous environmental factors that impinge on the patient.

In conjoint therapy the therapist finds himself in the same room (which somehow appears smaller) with *two* patients and with himself as a third patient. In other words, at the outset there are two intimates already maximally transferred to each other and minimally transferred to him. Symbolically, at least, there are three sets of parents in the room, theirs and mine, and perhaps also grandparents and other relatives and often one or more children. At first I felt as though I had been dropped as a participant into the second act of

18

a Shakespearian tragedy without having been given any lines to speak. I learned that interventions must be prompt, accurate and directed at disturbed communicational and interpersonal processes. In conjoint marital psychotherapy, what is being said is much less important than how, when, and why it is being said. Temptations to deal with content prematurely or to treat "the patient" in the presence of the "normal" spouse must, in general, be scrupulously avoided. Permitting oneself to become involved in a one-to-one interaction with either spouse is of no value and is actually a waste of time, unless the behavior is specifically planned in advance for a definite purpose. I found making the transition from what had become habitual and routine in individual psychotherapy a most difficult task, as it would be for any practitioner of individual psychotherapy whose training and experience had been along similar lines. Overseeing others who are beginning to conduct conjoint marital psychotherapy has definitely confirmed this conclusion.

My experience in the supervision of therapists, irrespective of their specific disciplines, indicates that, in general, group therapists have an easier time of it. They are already used to tuning out content much of the time and to dealing with disordered communications, small-group dynamics, and interpersonal processes. Most group therapists have already learned to avoid, or else to keep to a minimum, one-to-one therapist–patient interactions. They have less to unlearn and, hence, less of a difficult transition to make.

CHAPTER II

The Therapist as Travel Agent: Getting Therapy Started

I FREQUENTLY USE the analogy of the therapist as a travel agent, explaining to the couple that it is their responsibility to set their goals, while it is the therapist's to help them attain these goals. I give them my *opinion* about the feasibility and probability of their getting where they want to go, as well as point out the hazards they are likely to meet along the way and at their destination. Especially with couples in antagonistic marriages, where divorce is under consideration, I make it clear that the decision to stay together or divorce is theirs and theirs alone. The function of therapy is to provide fuller and deeper understanding, so that the decision they finally arrive at is more likely to be a more reasoned one. I frequently call to the patients' attention the clinically proven fact that human beings tend to repeat   21 their mistakes, unless, on their own or with the assistance of therapy, they have learned from them. I spell this out concretely, using an example like the following:

We are all too familiar with the tragic story of the woman whose first husband was an alcoholic. Her second turned out to be addicted to gambling and her third an embezzler. Unfortunately, she could not learn from her mistakes on her own. Something within her, a kind of self-defeating radar, continually drove her to choose a mate with some kind of defect in his personality. For many people changing partners completely fails to solve their problems.

In the interest of clarity, the therapist may make his values with respect to marriage explicit, but let me emphasize that under no circumstances should he advise for or against divorce. Furthermore, if divorce is decided upon, therapy need not end at the point where that decision is made. The couple frequently requires considerable assistance in disentangling from each other and in planning a divorce that is least painful for all concerned.

As with other forms of therapy, structuring is the first order of business in conjoint marital psychotherapy. Some structuring can, and indeed should, be done at the initial telephone contact. I answer my own telephone, with the aid of an automatic telephone-answering device, and arrange my own appointments. Thus, I have an early opportunity to determine the nature of the problem or problems that prompt the patient to seek an appointment in the first place and to ascertain the patient's marital status and family circumstances. I can then outline my routine procedure, that is, meeting with each spouse separately for a couple of sessions "so that I can get to know each of you as an individual, and give each of you the chance to get acquainted with me as an individual, before the three of us begin active therapy."

Where the presenting problem is with the marriage or with

a child or adolescent, the need for both spouses or parents to participate in therapy is self-evident, at least to those who have a modicum of motivation for this form of therapy. Only rarely—for example, in the case of an older or emancipated teenager—will I accept a case where the spouses are not willing to meet my conditions with respect to the attendance of both. In the case of an individual in a viable marriage seeking therapy for a nonmarital problem, I strongly urge the participation of the spouse, but I will accept the patient for individual psychotherapy. I have found most spouses surprisingly eager to enter therapy with the wife or husband who is asking for help; in my experience only 3 to 4 percent have opted against joining us.

There is a definite danger in sending a message to the other spouse through the one who has been interviewed. First, a straightforward invitation to the spouse to arrange an appointment is likely to become something like "The doctor thinks you're to blame for my troubles; he wants to see you." Or worse, "The doctor wants to see you; he thinks you're crazier than I am." It is much safer to lay the groundwork for the therapist's meeting with the spouse at the time of the first telephone contact. If, for some reason, this has not been done, it is then better to call the spouse oneself and to explain directly the reasons for wanting to see her or him. With those couples—and they are few—not expecting a recommendation for conjoint marital psychotherapy, I usually explain that I like to work with couples, since I believe that those who live intimately together have a great impact on each other and that when we're working on emotional problems, three heads are better than two. Any implication of blame or causality should, obviously, be carefully avoided. It would be a mistake to say, "You may be playing some role in your wife's illness." If the voice on the other end of the phone asks defensively, "Do you think that the trouble   23 is my fault?" the proper reply would be, "Certainly not. I need your help in searching for any factors that may be contributing to the trouble."

More often than not, when the presenting problem is with a child or a teen-ager, the mother makes the initial contact. In speaking with the father, it is important to emphasize the meaningfulness of his role in the family, as well as in the proposed therapy. My goal here is to structure the therapy so that some part of it turns out to be conjoint marital psychotherapy; the child or adolescent is dismissed as quickly as possible, taken into therapy individually, or else referred for peer-group therapy. The younger the child, the more likely my recommendation that the parents be treated instead of the child. If more child psychiatrists or analysts were available in our area, I would no doubt refer more youngsters than I do for their own treatment. I find, and the parents spontaneously report, that successful treatment of the parents regularly results in favorable changes in the child.

History Taking

In taking a history, many marriage therapists never, or only rarely, see the individual spouses separately; indeed, some do not take a history at all. I do not feel comfortable starting therapy cold without first gathering historical material from each spouse alone; this usually means two hours of individual interviewing for each before conjoint marital psychotherapy begins. When the identified patient is a teen-ager, I regularly see him or her alone for a session or two. Teen-agers have a private life apart from their family life and need to be offered an opportunity to discuss their problems within the context of a confidential relationship. This

is also designed to build some measure of trust and rapport before the adolescent is seen together with his parents or family. With each spouse the history-taking process varies from the standard clinical interview only in emphasis and focus.

In the first part of the interview, which is ordinarily devoted to the present and the more immediate past, questions are raised about mate selection. By this I do not mean merely factual material or a recounting of the sequence of events of the courtship but also, and more importantly, memories about what attracted one to the other and kept them interested in each other, with special attention to the feelings involved. I am also interested in the person's impressions of what it was about him or herself that attracted and kept the spouse interested. These are frequently difficult questions for patients to answer, so that some pressing and probing becomes necessary. I find myself urging the patient to turn his imagination loose and to guess at what may have been the case at the time the mate selection was going on. Obviously the memories elicited are likely to be conscious ones, and they are also apt to be contaminated by what has occurred between that past and the present. Even so, it may be possible to arrive at some inferences about less conscious attitudes and motivations. If a wife recalls with pleasure and admiration her husband's quiet, reserved, polite, and unaggressive attitude toward physical contact, it is not difficult to infer that her prospective spouse did not at that time threaten her defenses against sexuality. When a man emphasizes sympathy and the ability to listen to and understand his problems on the part of his wife-to-be, the therapist may suspect that the husband was looking for someone to fulfill his leftover childhood longings for mothering. It is well to keep in mind that the young man or woman may have been seeing the spouse-to-be through a fantasy 25 of his needs and ignoring qualities that contradicted this romantic hope. Smoke does indeed get into one's eyes, as an insightful lyricist informed us years ago.

A detailed history of the patient's sex life, both past and present, should be elicited. I try to probe the patient's memories of the attitudes and feelings that existed in his childhood home concerning sexual matters. And I ask the patient to guess what his parents' love life may have been like. Special attention is given to the patient's experiences with adolescent masturbation, and I raise this issue with both women and men. Again, eliciting feelings and attitudes is more important than facts, although it is of some significance when one encounters a man who never, or only rarely, was able to permit himself to masturbate. Certain questions are important: How do you recall feeling about your masturbating? Do you remember any feelings of guilt or shame, fear or worry? Did it bother you so much that you struggled against the urge to do so, vowed never to do it again, and then felt badly when you succumbed to the desire? With a woman it is important to ascertain if she knew about menstruation before she had her first period. Who told her about it and how? If her mother talked with her about it, how did the mother seem to feel? Was she adequately and reassuringly informed about the subject? What was her emotional reaction when her first period actually started? And did her parents seem to treat her any differently after the event than before? When the interviewer is able to approach this subject in a casual, matter-of-fact way, most patients are able to be open and honest about their sexual practices and the feelings associated with them. The patient may question the use the therapist will make of the information the patient is about to reveal or whether it will be necessary to share everything with the spouse during the course of therapy. It is essential to reassure the patient that the therapist in
no sense acts as a transmitter of information and that it is

the patient—and no one else—who will determine what he will or will not discuss. Furthermore, if and when the question should arise, it must be made clear that under no circumstances will the therapist participate in any legal proceedings whatsoever—separation, divorce, child custody, or anything else.

On three or four occasions this contract has not been respected by patients who have decided upon divorce, and I have received a call from an attorney: "Doctor, you treated a patient, Mrs. Mary Smith, about a year ago. She is now my client and is divorcing her husband. I would like you to testify in her divorce (or child custody or other) hearing on her behalf." At first I usually reply, "That would be contrary to my policy and to the agreement reached with both husband and wife during their therapy with me. All the information I have was gathered within a therapy situation. It would prejudice my position with my present and future patients were I to use such information for any other purpose than a therapeutic one." If the attorney persists I add, "There is a question here of what constitutes informed consent. Neither you nor Mrs. Smith knows all that may have to be included in my testimony. What I may have to say could work against her in terms of your goals." If he presses the issue further, I continue, "I'm sure, Mr. Jones, that you know from experience what kind of trouble you could have with a hostile witness if you force me to testify by having a subpoena issued. In any event I shall not do so voluntarily." I know that I am on somewhat shaky ground here. It is my understanding that in most states that have a statute bearing upon privileged communication between physician and patient, the physician's statutory protection is vitiated by the presence of a third party during the interview. It is crucial to know the essential difference between "privileged communication," a legal concept, and "confidentiality," which arises from ethical considerations. Put to the test on   *27* the issue of confidentiality, I would have to give priority to ethical considerations for the welfare of all my patients, past, present, and future, and refuse to testify even at the risk of being cited for contempt of court. Other therapists will have to make their own decision about the ethics involved.

In the second part of the interview, special attention is directed to the patient's relationships—their nature, quality, and the feelings involved—with his parents and siblings during the various phases of his psychological development. Discipline, parental expectations, and demands on behavior deserve special attention. Which of these matters was especially important to the parent or parents, and what measures were used to enforce their wishes or demands? Was there agreement between the parents concerning them? Memories of how the patient reacted to the parents' notions of "correct" behavior and the parents' reaction to the child's nonconformity with these ideas are important. In other words, was the child tractable or rebellious? Further, I make a definite effort to obtain as much information as I can about the marriage model or models that the patient directly observed and experienced during childhood, especially the feelings that he sensed between the parental couple or couples and how those feelings were manifested. For instance, a young man describes his memories of his parents as follows:

I can't recall my parents ever having had an argument. If they did, they never did so in front of us. They never had a cross word. My mother was a quiet person who respected my father; he made all of the decisions. She went along with all of his wishes. If she ever disagreed she must have kept it to herself, because we never heard of any disagreement from her.

Such a story leads me to speculate that this man, as a husband, will probably be extremely sensitive about any assertiveness on the part of his wife. He will expect her to keep her proper place and perhaps be offended if she merely offers an opinion or makes a suggestion.

Other Information Gathering

Those therapists who find earliest memories and dreams —recent, past, repetitive, or nightmares—useful in preparing for other forms of psychotherapy will find them equally useful in preparing to undertake conjoint marital therapy. One may be fortunate enough to encounter dreams reported by both that seem to be reactive to a shared life event. Inferences can then be drawn as to the individual reactions to that event, as well as to its less conscious impact on, and meaning within, the relationship. This can enhance the therapist's understanding and often proves useful. To illustrate, a husband reported a dream on the night he had an unsuccessful sexual experience in which he lost his erection before penetration: "I was living in the country and I came upon a farm which had a fence around part of the yard. An Irish setter was guarding the gate. He seemed unfriendly." On the same night the wife dreamed: "A carpenter was working in our house repairing something. He dropped his hammer and it made a dent in our new tile floor." The associations each had to their respective dreams, which were thinly disguised in the first place, led me to understand that both were fearful of penetration, he of hurting, she of being hurt. Depending upon the circumstances and the phase of therapy, I may or may not impart this understanding to the couple. In the earliest stage of treatment, particularly if other problems deserve higher priority, I might not ask for associations at all.

In gathering this kind of information about the patients, my aim is to help formulate a tentative picture of the dynamics and genetics of each spouse as an individual, as well as *29* the probable transferences, defenses, conflicts, complementarities, and dissonances in their marital relationship. Since much of what occurs between a couple occurs outside of their awareness (because of their closeness to the action and to the distorting effect of intense emotion), there is often a great discrepancy between what a couple tell me about their relationship and what I am able to observe directly while they are interacting in my presence. What I have in mind is the patient who describes his or her spouse as a very stubborn and unyielding person, totally unaware that he or she manifests these same characteristics in marital interactions. This patient may respond to a position taken by the spouse by exclaiming, "You always want and get your way! This is one time I'm not going to give in," proving to be just as unyielding. Every discussion in which there is a difference of opinion ends in a "Mexican standoff." Nevertheless, such a patient may interact differently with me.

I realize that my presence and interventions may change the very character of a couple's interactions in some measure. However, I have the distinct impression that most couples "forget" my presence, once I have withdrawn to the position of quiet observer, and that they then "go at it" with each other as they do at home.

In the initial history-gathering interviews I maintain relatively tight control over the course and direction of the interview. In this way I am able to obtain as much relevant data as possible in the shortest possible time. If they are permitted to do so, patients may wander indiscriminately or may relate the history in an overly detailed manner, thus avoiding painful, embarrassing, or humiliating material.

For a brief time near the end of the interview, I do encourage more free-wheeling, free-associative type of communication. I also invite the patient to raise whatever questions he would like me to reply to. I may also share tentative formulations with the patient, being careful to label these as hypothetical, speculative, or educated guesses. For example, I may say,

Based on what you have told me about yourself up to this point, I have developed a couple of tentative impressions or hunches about you. Please bear in mind that I have known you for a very short time, so that I could be inaccurate. But what I have to say is also based on my knowledge about and experience with many other people. I suspect that you are extremely sensitive about the possibility of losing any person who comes to be important to you. In your childhood you lost your grandmother; you and she had been very close, and that hit you very hard. Then when you were fourteen you lost both of your parents in that automobile accident, and that too was a terrible blow to you. Such experiences often leave a person with forebodings about the possible repetition of losing a person to whom he becomes closely attached. I suspect that this leads you to be worried about losing your wife, and this, in turn, leads you to watch over her very closely. This may have some kind of an effect on her not desired by you and may be causing some trouble between you.

Note that I offer this interpretation carefully, in the form of a trial balloon, giving the patient ample room to reject it. Many patients are able to accept and benefit from such an explanation, even at this early time in our relationship. If I feel the patient may not be able to "take it," however tactfully the information may be offered, I reserve comment. (See Appendix A: Illustrative Case History.)

At this point we are ready to begin our first conjoint marital therapy session.

The First Conjoint Session

It is at the beginning of this interview that the patient –therapist contract with respect to fees and cancellations is set forth and agreed upon, if this has not already been done. The couple are also informed that from this point forward the therapy is a joint one and that the therapist will not meet with either of them alone, unless the three of us have, in advance, agreed to change the treatment plan. The occasions are rare, indeed, when I agree to see the spouse who arrives alone, other than to ascertain whether or not the absence of the other has been necessitated by reality factors. About this, I am very strict. When one spouse is absent for obviously illegitimate or suspiciously weak reasons, it almost always represents a collusive ploy, with any number of possible underlying motivations. After a brief discussion, the one who has arrived alone under such questionable circumstances is sent away with the expressed expectation that the *three* of us are to meet next week at the regular time.

One example of the above maneuver is significant enough to be mentioned. In the case of a wife who has been or is involved in a real or fantasied extramarital relationship, couples frequently attempt to act out the triangular drama with the male therapist in the role of the symbolic "boyfriend." The therapist must be alert to this; it is also possible that a female therapist may substitute for a "girlfriend." When, for some legitimate reason, one spouse is seen alone, the focus should definitely be restricted to the patient present. Any comments made about the absent spouse should never, to any degree, be "negative." It must be borne constantly in mind that when any patient is talking about someone else, he may be dealing with a hated, denied, and projected aspect of himself, though he himself may be completely unaware of this.

In introducing the therapy to the couple, I offer the following explanations and directives:

32   1. The treatment interviews will be entirely different from

the initial ones in that I shall be in the position of an observer much of the time.

2. I need to listen to them as they talk mainly *to each other* so that I have the opportunity to watch, listen, and think. This allows me to arrive at understandings hidden from them because of their closeness to themselves ("not being able to see the forest for the trees" or "emotional smoke gets in your eyes").

3. They are free to start where they wish and also to choose the topics for discussion or argument.

4. As far as is humanly possible, I shall endeavor not to take sides. This, however, does not necessarily mean complete moment-to-moment neutrality but rather neutrality over the long haul.

5. If I seem to them to violate the above commitment in any way, I trust they will feel free to call this to my attention so that I can objectively, in the light of their view or views, examine my own feelings and behavior.

6. If the question of probable length of treatment has not been covered with both in the individual interviews, I introduce it. Since the average length of treatment for those who become meaningfully involved has proven to be about six months, I state this as a *statistical* fact. But I also explain that this figure includes some couples with minor difficulties who completed therapy within a much shorter period of time and also some couples who required a little over two years of treatment. The length of therapy is very difficult to predict until the three of us have an opportunity to determine the depth and complexity of their individual or joint problems. In the case of patients who have entered conjoint therapy for a problem that they regard as unrelated to their marriage or family life, avoiding implications of causality or blame is especially important. Contracts regarding the length of therapy are obviously not enforceable, but such a time frame helps a couple in their budgetary and other   *33*

planning and helps to modify any unrealistic anticipations.

7. "Anything goes—except breaking up the furniture." This, by humorous implication, tells the couple that any and all physical violence is completely forbidden. In cases where violence has actually occurred or has been threatened, or where, in my judgment, it is a possibility, I make it part of the treatment contract that lethal weapons—especially guns that are owned—must be disposed of or put in the care of a trusted other so that they will not be readily available.

Obviously, all elements of the contract that might be established and the directives that might be given the couple are not necessarily appropriate in every single instance; they must be specifically tailored to fit the particular conditions that exist. If, for example, the couple are unaware of any marital problem at the outset, although I may have spotted one or more, the question of taking sides would not seem to them to be pertinent and yet it definitely would be. On the theory that it is "better to have it and not need it, than to need it and not have it," it is a good idea to have the directives cover rather wide territory.

Common Problems

Many years ago I took horseback riding lessons from an exceptionally wise animal trainer, who very quickly taught me that I—not the horse—was the animal most likely to be the problem. If leaning slightly forward in the saddle, loosening the reins, and gently abducting the thighs against the horse's body were enough to get the horse going, more strenuous measures were unnecessary. On the other hand, some horses might require a digging in of the spurs, accompanied by a sharp blow with one's riding crop. To become 34 a skillful rider one must learn how and when to use which tactic and all the steps in between. Such wisdom and sensitivity to the temperament of the other are no less useful characteristics for the psychotherapist to have or to develop.

It hardly seems necessary to add to the volumes that have been written about dealing with the patient's silences in the therapeutic interview. Only rarely, however, in conjoint marital psychotherapy, do both patients simultaneously feel so frightened, angry, hopeless, embarrassed, or whatever, that they both remain silent at the same time; thus, silence is much less often a problem. When it does occur, it is dealt with no differently than it is in individual psychotherapy. Each patient's talking mainly with the therapist is often an early problem, since this is a way of masking communicational and transactional processes that exist between the spouses. One or the other or both in turn offer the therapist temptingly juicy material, to which it would be easy for him to respond in a one-to-one relationship. An attractive young woman in an early conjoint session may say, for example, "I don't see any harm in being a little flirtatious; I'm a friendly person. But John gets insanely jealous when I do. Isn't it normal, Doctor, for a woman to kid around some with other men?" I reply, "That's between you and John. What's normal, *if* I knew—and I do *not*—doesn't make any difference. Let me hear you discuss it with him." Only in exceptional instances does it prove fruitful to permit the therapy to proceed with the patient's speaking to or through the therapist, although at times it may be necessary for a short period. Certainly when the marriage or a child is the "identified patient," this procedure is rarely productive.

From the beginning I attempt to turn the flow of the interview around by remaining silent myself, acting bored, looking at neither spouse directly. I just await their first addressing comments to each other. At point I may move in with some supportive comment, such as: "Now you're cooking; that's what I need to hear." Perhaps a patient, addressing me, will say that just yesterday he told his wife that if she'd get out of the house more, it would help her stop washing her hands fifty times a day. I then invite the husband to say it again, right then, in front of me, just the way he did yesterday, so that I can see what will happen.

If, however, these maneuvers do not work, I may confront the couple with their apparent inability or unwillingness to follow my directions. I inquire whether they have any idea what is blocking them from doing so. If I have any insight, gleaned from the original diagnostic interviews, as to the dynamic source of their difficulty, I try to interpret the source of their anxiety or else comment, for example, on their characterological stubbornness and seek, or even suggest to them, its possible genetic origins.

It may appear that most of my interventions are directed toward the couple, that is, to the two of them. This is by no means the case, however. Interpretations that I make to one spouse (judged at the moment to be more receptive or less vulnerable) are obviously heard by the other as well. What may appear on the surface in one could, and often does, exist in the depth of the other as well. If a wife is one millimeter neater, cleaner, and more orderly than her husband, his anxiety in this area will never become evident. If a husband's social anxiety keeps the couple at home all the time, avoiding social situations, the wife's similar anxiety will never become a problem for her. A husband may pamper his wife's fear of open streets because he too has an unconscious fantasy—arising, perhaps, out of his feeling that he is not sexually adequate enough to hold her—that she may not be faithful to him.

In the interest of balance and in keeping my bargain concerning neutrality, I make a concerted effort to address an equal number of "with-the-stream" (ego-syntonic) and "against-the-stream" (ego-alien) comments, questions, confrontations, or interpretations to each at every session. An example of the first would be, "Most people require confirmation of worth from someone important to them sometimes." An example of the second kind would be, "Your need to give gratuitous advice is certainly abrasive." Exceptions to this practice do occur, especially in the later phases of therapy.

One spouse may talk so much and the other so little that this actually represents a communicational problem and also allows the silent one to hide behind the verbiage of the other. Again the therapist may try certain gentle, or even more forceful, manipulations: encouraging the more quiet one, urging them to take turns so that they have more equal time, blocking out the overtalkative one either verbally or nonverbally. Sometimes I suggest to one spouse, "Why don't you and I keep quiet and give John a chance to have something bubble up from within him that he would like to talk about?" On the other hand, if the therapist knows or strongly suspects the underlying reasons for the defense shown in this over- or undertalkativeness, he may first try the interpretative route. This circumstance may present, on the surface, a communicational vicious circle: The more one spouse talks, the more silent the other becomes; the more silent he is, the more agitated and talkative the other grows. Thus, each pushes the other progressively deeper into silent communicational modes or into excessively talkative ones. This vicious circle must then be spelled out to the couple by the therapist in terms they can grasp.

It is useful to think of the therapeutic process in terms of phases or priorities: Serious communicational problems preempt dealing with transactional problems. These, in turn, preempt dealing with intrapsychic dynamics; from accurate interpretation of the latter follows the diminution of interfering transferences and defensiveness in the relationship. This, in its turn, leads to increased understanding, acceptance, 37 and empathy. Such a mode of thinking is not useful when the attempt is made to apply it in practice, cookbook fashion, step by step. It becomes valuable, however, when the discussion has become so chaotic as to be massively confusing. (See Appendix C, Interviews 1 and 2, for an example.) Nothing can be accomplished until the couple is assisted over this first hurdle.

Abuse of the agenda, whether it occurs in therapy or at a committee or board meeting, can lead only to disorganization and the failure to resolve any issue whatsoever. The effective therapist, like an effective chairman, must be permissive enough to hear out each individual but strong enough to keep the discussion on the target, even if not precisely on the bull's-eye. One of the most common and easy-to-spot forms of abuse of the agenda is the drastic change of subject. Thus, the couple will move rapidly from issue A to issue B to issue C, and so on, *ad infinitum.* When I discern this pattern, I move in on it promptly and firmly, much as the chairman of a meeting rules a motion out of order or informs the speaker that he is not addressing himself to the issue at hand. Doing so once is never sufficient, however. The therapist will find that he must again and again insist that issue B is out of order until issue A is disposed of.

Another common form of agenda abuse might more properly be called drifting or sliding subtly away from the subject. The therapist may have the mistaken impression that the couple are still talking about the same thing. For example, a disagreement about a prospective trip may drift into a discussion of buying this or that type of tent before any decision has been reached on whether to go. I frequently have to bring the couple back by injecting: "Did you get an answer to that question you raised ten minutes ago about whether to take the trip?" or "You began talking about X, and now you're talking about Y. What happened? How did you get from there to here?"

Sometimes couples demonstrate their caution with each other, or their need to avoid a confrontation, by keeping their discussion on an overly abstract level. To the therapist they sound like diplomats making statements for public consumption. Confronting them with how they sound, urging them to be more specific, pressing for examples, or explaining why they seem to need to communicate in this manner are some of the options open to the therapist. With the many patients who tend to intellectualize, colloquial language, sometimes even slang or four-letter words, may prove effective.

Recently, when it has seemed to me that patients continue overlong without opening up to each other and other measures have failed to alter this situation, I have experimented with the following procedure: I ask them to write letters to each other. Either one may take the initiative in writing the first letter. The other is to read and think about the letter he or she receives and then reply after two or three days. I do this when I know from individual sessions or intuit that one or the other or both are avoiding an anticipated disaster of some kind by pussyfooting in their verbal communications. Most couples have exchanged letters, especially during their courtship, and I remind them of this: The letters are in some sense to be "love letters" but should also contain some meaningful feelings, attitudes, gripes, or hopes they have been unable to talk about. (See Appendix B for two actual, appropriately disguised letters.) This device has served to break the communicational log jam several times.

In my supervision of others, I have noticed a common tendency among therapists to communicate on the same level as the patient; this only seems to reinforce the defense that is being engaged in. Analogies or metaphors, however, should definitely be pitched at the patient's level of understanding. A person with limited intellectual powers or the 39 absence of technical education would be unlikely to grasp a thermodynamic analogy, unless it was put in such simple terms as a water tank with a plugged safety valve. I do not feel right in using the idiosyncratic language of my younger patients—for example, "rip off" for "steal"; it seems an affront to my generational individuality, and I expect I would sound phony to myself and undoubtedly even more so to them.

So much has been written by experts in communicational processes about incongruities between levels of communication that I do not need to repeat or review their work here. I have already stressed the importance of the therapist's keeping his actions consistent with his words and of the various forms of nonverbal behavior as well. A high degree of self-awareness is vital. Fortunately, there are devices available to therapists for checking on themselves and sharpening their self-awareness:

1. The therapist may listen to and view himself either alone or in the company of a colleague or colleagues by the use of audio- or videotapes.

2. Therapists may occasionally or regularly work in a co-therapy situation, so that they can help each other with any possible slips of their communicational, and perhaps also other, gears.

3. The therapist may conduct therapy sessions with an audience in the room or behind a one-way mirror.

It ought not be necessary to add (but, unfortunately, it is) that the tape recorder or the mirror should be used only with the knowledge and consent of the involved patients. Such permission is seldom difficult to obtain if the therapist is at peace with himself as far as exposing his work to himself and to others. Most of the time patients react positively if the therapist is able to broach the subject in a matter-of-fact, casual manner. Some patients may require the reassurance that the device is being used for self-study. If others beside the therapist and the couple are to participate, the therapist may say something like: "You don't have to worry about them; they will be watching or listening to me, not examining or judging you."

In treating couples one may confidently expect to find varying degrees of incongruent verbal/nonverbal communicational difficulties. These definitely require treatment. A demand for more accurate or detailed terminology might train the couple to become more conscious of their own and each other's communicational patterns and problems. I frequently bring up the following types of questions, comments, or confrontations:

What would your hand (or foot) say right now if it could talk?

Have you noticed that your husband sounds perfectly calm but that he seems to be squirming?

From what you're saying now I would expect you to look and/or sound angry, but to me it sounds as though you were referring to something as inconsequential as a change in the weather.

Every time your wife begins to weep, I notice that you look out of the window; let's see what would happen if you were to watch her. Isn't it interesting that you were able to look at her for no more than a split second? Do either of you have any idea what that means?

Your words sound like insults, but your face gives me the impression that you are telling a joke. Which is it? Which do you really mean?

Are you aware that while you were saying that, your fist was clenched so that your knuckles showed white?

You seemed to me to be blushing just then, but that's the only indication I had that my remark had embarrassed you.

Your hand moved two inches closer to his (her) shoulder, then stopped abruptly. Were you aware of that? What happened?

Let me again point out that I may address myself to either one or to both and that I signal which I am doing verbally or nonverbally. Some of the above remarks point out more than communicational difficulties, of course. For instance, the patient who moved his hand closer to his spouse and then abruptly stopped encountered anxiety, and stopping allayed this fear. Perhaps the anxiety relates to the expression of tender feelings; perhaps it arises from a fear of rejection. The source of this anxiety, signaled by stopping (or looking out of the window) requires exploration at the earliest possible moment.

Another common form of difficulty appears in the verbal content of the messages: A patient may take away in the second half of a sentence or paragraph what he has just given in the first; his ambivalence may be blatant to the therapist. For example, a patient may say to his or her spouse, "Yes, you *did* remember my birthday, but it was at the *last* minute!" Usually the spouse hears only the second half of the message, the first half having gotten drowned out. In this way the true psychological value of what is said never gets through. When the receiver of the message responds to its negative part, he commonly does so either defensively or as a counterattack; negatives escalate. The therapist's task is to help the couple keep the positives separate from the negatives or, as I often put it, to put the periods where they belong, instead of overusing semicolons. I may concretize and further dramatize this by vigorously inserting, "Period!" at the proper place, by signaling, "Stop!" like the traffic cop on the corner, or, more gently, by warning, "Be careful, now, or you'll be in the soup again."

I mention the next commonly occurring phenomenon here because it manifests itself early in the treatment, not because it is strictly communicational in nature. One or the other patient, or both, may block the therapist out of his role by analyzing the other, instead of permitting the therapist to do this. The therapist may overcome this type of maneuver by the strategies already mentioned.

Once these interferences with clear message receiving and sending have been successfully treated, they occur less and less frequently, and the first phase of therapy has, in the main, been concluded. This is not to say that the same or similar problems do not ever arise. Now, however, the patients catch themselves falling into these binds and get themselves back on the right track with minimal or no assistance.

The therapist is then ready to turn his attention to other troublesome aspects of the relationship. A few words about terminating therapy interviews are appropriate here. If at all possible, I prefer to have the session end on some kind of positive, or at least neutral, note. So, I watch the clock. About ten minutes before the time is up, I try to find or create something hopeful or encouraging to comment upon. Lacking this, I try to slow down the action, stop the fight, and encourage some reflection about what has occurred in the session or how they feel about what has happened. I may offer a summary and even suggest that they give some thought to it later. Alternatively, I may say, for example, "You two can sure arouse intense feelings in each other, which proves that you're far from indifferent, one to the other."

CHAPTER III

In the Jungle:
The Middle Phase
of Therapy

*N*OW THAT the landscape is no longer obscured by communicational fog, other obstacles to marital and personal growth become evident with ever greater clarity. The following categories of material emerge and need to be tackled therapeutically: transactional or interactional material; transferential material; defensive material; dynamic material; and genetic material. When therapist and couple have succeeded in working through this material, increased acceptance, understanding, and empathy follow; symptoms and symptomatic behavior concomitantly decrease. Such improvement occurs in both the marital unit and in each spouse as an individual. Occasionally, after completion of conjoint marital psychotherapy, one spouse may feel the need of additional personal therapy, and the therapist may feel this is indicated.

Process Focus versus Content Focus

I have mentioned the value of focusing on process rather than content, but how is this to be accomplished? With today's overemphasis on sexual matters, it would be all too easy for me (or any other therapist) to plunge precipitously into a discussion of the mechanics of the couple's sexual activity. Doing so this early in the game, however, will hide more than it will reveal.

What is important is how the couple deal with each other as they talk about sex or any other subject. Let me cite some common examples: As the couple talk about a particular subject, the therapist observes that one spouse repeatedly appears impatient, intolerant, and bossy, while the other sounds angry, rebellious, and resistive. Symptomatically, these former qualities may be expressed in an obsessive–compulsive form. An extreme instance is the husband who insisted that his wife wash their undergarments and handkerchiefs separately from the rest of their clothing and that she wash their child's toys three times a day—in the interest of their health! Expressed behaviorally, the rebellious spouse may be acting out against the controlling one by arriving home two hours later than expected, by drinking to excess, by spending money extravagantly, or through extramarital relations, to cite a few very common examples.

In place of responding to *what* the couple are talking about, the therapist responds to and comments on the nature of their interactions or transactions. I ask if they know how they sound to me; often they reply "silly" or "like two kids." They are almost always quite unaware how I have been perceiving them. I turn to one and say, for example, "You sound like an exasperated parent trying to control a rebellious teen-ager." To the other I add, "And you sound like a rebellious teen-ager trying to outmaneuver a stern parent. Now I don't know whether you're treating her like this because she's acting that way, or whether you're acting like this because he's treating you that way." Even those patients who are able to agree quickly, and to talk about how they sound and why, can seldom continue for more than several sen-tences before they are once more pulled back into the same interactional trap. I call this to their attention by saying, "See how compelling this is for you; even when you make the effort and try not to do what has just been pointed out to you, here you are again, back in the same pattern."

Another familiar example is the couple operating at the extreme poles of the dependency–independency continnum. One spouse may seem strong, decisive, assertive, and sure of himself, while the other characterizes all the antonyms of these adjectives. When the latter spouse has been driven to a symptomatic expression of these traits, they may appear in his case as anxious, phobic, or depressive states. One shouldn't be fooled into believing that the weaker one needs the therapist's support against the "aggressive monster." In a dyad, the power is usually equally divided, although it is frequently differently expressed. The meek do inherit their share of the earth!

It is interesting to observe what happens—especially if the "more independent" spouse has been critical of the other's dependence—when the therapist points out the indomitable strength in apparent weakness: "You get your way just as often as he gets his, maybe even more often." "You pushed him into making that decision by pretending that you weren't able to. What a power play!" "Are you aware how adroitly he gets you to do his bidding?" With these remarks the therapist avoids being drawn into commenting on the merits of the issues and has sought to give the couple a new and 47 different perspective on themselves. One or the other may then attempt a change. Perhaps the "weaker" one tries being a bit assertive, saying: "I'd rather go out to dinner tonight," whereupon the spouse blows his stack. This gives me the opportunity to point out: "Just a minute, there. Hold on. It was my understanding, and I thought I had heard you say eighteen times, that you wanted *her* to make just one decision or to express just one preference. That's just what she's done now, and look how you reacted! How come? Do you know?"

Each spouse blaming the other is also a common enough pattern of interaction to deserve mention: "You did (or said) this." "Yes, I did, but you did (or said) that, and that's worse." Characteristically, both these patients operate under a chronic and overweening burden of self-criticism. One blames the other because he feels a blame within himself; by ascribing the fault to the spouse, it becomes confirmed and amplified in the spouse. Unable to forgive himself for his own short-comings or limitations, each patient finds himself unable to forgive the other; neither can help the other spouse to modify the degree of guilt they both share. The therapist, of course, must avoid judging the topics under discussion, although the couple repeatedly offer him implicit, tacit, or even open invitations to do just that. Comments are to be directed at the process.

In this type of situation, I have found several kinds of intervention helpful:

1. Pointing out how they keep tossing a big black ball of blame back and forth as though it were in a game of "catch."

2. Asking what would be accomplished if I could, with scientific precision, weigh the exact amount of blame and assign, for example, three ounces to one and three and a half ounces to the other.

3. Explaining the essential difference between guilt and responsibility and illustrating this by saying, for instance, "Whatever happens in this room among the three of us is like an equation, a times b times c equals z. If we succeed, we do so together, the three of us; and the same holds true if we fail. Since I am the professional involved, I am always ready to take 40 percent of the responsibility."

4. Expressing compassionate concern about the pain they are experiencing.

5. Robbing the blame of its significance by labeling it futile, a waste of time, oriented only to the past, and unable to help in solving present problems.

6. Suggesting the cultural basis for learning this process: Their parents may have been more interested in finding out who started a fight than in stopping it.

Intuition, tact, and his own feelings are the only guides the therapist has to fall back on in matching couple to the tactic. A certain amount of trial and error is necessary.

Doing something to stop repetitive blaming is unquestionably better than doing nothing. My main aim, however, is to emphasize the importance of dealing with behavior, as opposed to subject matter. It is seldom possible to get beneath the blaming process until the process itself has been modified or interrupted. When one spouse has already collapsed under the weight of this mutual torture, the symptomatic patient may present as depressed or obsessive–compulsive. In such cases the blaming has become more covert, and therapy has to start at a different place. After the therapist has translated the symptom back into relationship terms, however, the same or a similar tactical approach remains efficacious.

How does the therapist translate symptoms or symptomatic behavior back into relationship terms? Put simply, by observing and attempting to understand the symptoms as they occur naturally and spontaneously in the course of the

49

therapy session. What is going on between the patients when a symptom occurs or is mentioned? Alternatively, what leads to a change in the opposite direction, when, for example, the sad patient brightens up somewhat? How the patient uses the symptom in the context of the relationship is paramount here. As soon as the therapist spots a pattern or becomes aware of what is going on, he is in a position to make the couple aware of it.

A patient may use symptoms to control; to get even; to make the spouse feel guilty, ashamed, or anxious; or to preserve the relationship. The last item may seem paradoxical. I have in mind collusive arrangements where the "sick" spouse needs to remain sick so as not to threaten the "healthy" one. Though a husband may appear to be pressing forcefully for a healthier wife, at the first sign of improvement, he does something to sabotage it. A wife may ardently express her desire that her husband be more sexually potent—but the moment he becomes even a bit more assertive in the therapy interview, she becomes anxious and beats him down. The control aspect in the following therapy interview interchange is obvious:

Husband: I think it's time that I turn more of the responsibility for the grocery shopping over to you. You could go to the store with one of your friends or shop by phone. It's taking too much of my time away from the office and other things.

Wife: You know I'm too scared to ride in a car with anyone but you; I couldn't make it with one of my friends. And you also know that I wouldn't buy food without looking it over. I wouldn't feel right about shopping by phone.

Husband: Well, maybe we can work it out so that we do the shopping evenings or Saturday afternoons, so I don't lose time from work.

(Guilt arousal and resulting control aspects are also obvious in this exchange.)

Wife: Jane has invited me to spend the afternoon and evening with her in Detroit next Friday, and I've been thinking of taking her up on it.
Husband: (Drops his head. His facial expression changes from neutral to sad and sulky. He remains silent.)
Wife: I know it upsets you if I'm away when you're home, so maybe just the day would be enough.

Before deeper-level dynamics can be effectively approached, these secondary-gain phenomena must be successfully handled.

Interview Behavior Focus versus Related Behavior Focus

Implied but not explicated in the previous section is my preference for focusing on and dealing with what occurs in the here-and-now of the interview, rather than what is reported to have happened at home or elsewhere in the past. Between the incident and its recounting the patients utilize every possible defensive maneuver to distort the picture. I invite the couple, then and there, to reargue the issue in my presence, not to tell me what yesterday's argument was about. I may explain that I am unable to comment on something that I did not myself witness or experience. Or I may use one or several of the tactics previously discussed— silence, praise, criticism, or interpretation—to help the couple become less defensive. Lest my use of criticism be misinterpreted, some explanation is in order. I say, for example, 51

"Sinking, as you are, in the swamp of the past is both futile and ridiculous. If we could know with absolute certainty exactly who said or did what to whom and in what sequence, that and twenty cents would get us a cup of coffee in most restaurants." To a man who has just completely missed a peace offering from his wife, I may comment, "You have just won the Shithead of the Week award." I tell him why. To a woman I might say, "If you were my wife and you treated me like you just treated him, I'd feel like giving you a karate chop across your liver." Note that this kind of criticism contains some facetiousness to take the edge off of it.

Only when the defenses have softened and the couple are genuinely attempting to explore and unravel a problematic situation in the past, does it become expeditious to join them in their search for understanding. When the patients substantially agree as to the sequence of events and each is receptive to examining his own role in the relationship snarl, defensive softening has already taken place: "I was in a bad mood when I arrived home from the office, and I guess I couldn't listen to what you were saying." At this point it is helpful to explain how commonplace and inevitable conflicting needs between intimates can be and frequently are. For example, an exhausted and irritable husband arrives home in need of solitude at the very time when his wife, bored and enervated with child care and household chores, needs her husband's supportive companionship. I like to use the analogy of the decompression chamber required by the deep-sea diver, after he reaches the surface following a dive:

I have a fantasy; in every American home in which the man of the family has a responsible, difficult job there ought to be a decompression chamber just inside the door. It should be like the chamber deep-sea divers use when they come up from a dive into the ocean. Many men need some time to decompress, unwind, or put themselves back together, putting their career problems somewhat behind them, before they have to face their family problems.

Sometimes this explanation suffices. At other times, the couple may have to devise, or I may have to suggest, ways in which the couple could minimize such conflicts. This is one of the many times self-revelation on the part of the therapist can be beneficial. I might comment, "I could easily get into a big donnybrook with my wife at an occasion like this, if I didn't immediately explain and label my mood after a bad day. She might inadvertently say just the thing that could provoke me to dump all my garbage on her—most unfairly." To suggest solutions to some couples prematurely, however, is dangerous in terms of fostering undue dependency on the therapist. Making such suggestions inappropriately—that is, when the couple has not yet shown itself to be incapable of finding solutions—could represent a vote of no confidence by the therapist. A patient may say, "O.K., now we see the problem, but we need your help in finding an answer. Could you give us some direction?" I respond, "It would be much better if you could find your own solutions; then you will own them. And searching for them together is good practice in teamwork. To give you some advice or direction at this point would deprive you of the opportunity to use your own muscles and might, in effect, be a vote of no confidence in you on my part." Most couples do, indeed, engage in their own creative problem solving. Only a very few require direct suggestions, because of the limited behavioral repertoire available to them. If possible, however, I prefer to guide through example, as opposed to precept, indirectly and subtly, rather than directly.

Past, Present, and Future

Many couples are mired in the swamp of the past. They   53

must be helped to find their way into the present so that they can project themselves into the future. I make a definite effort to help the couple use the past in a constructive way. I explain to them that history cannot be rewritten, as politicians are wont to do, nor can history be changed. The only productive use of the past is for understanding the present and for planning for the future. "Forgetting it" or "starting over" are not solutions, since these are both impossible; the slate cannot be wiped clean. I convey these notions to the couple by precept and example. I insist firmly that the couple reargue the subject at issue in the interview, rather than recount the argument they had in the past, even when it is something they have already argued a hundred times before. That the issue or issues remain unresolved is sufficient evidence that the couple need assistance with the unsettled dispute. They must be taught how to fight better, how to win, how to give in and to lose, how to compromise, or how to devise policies for the future, so that each new situation does not have to be approached *ad hoc*. I have found that even a relatively simple thing like helping the couple agree and establish a contract that neither will spend more than a certain amount without checking it out with the other can avert considerable future trouble.

At the risk of sounding repetitious, let me again emphasize that I am not advocating a formalized, lockstep therapeutic process in which first this kind of material is handled, next that kind, and so on. In any one therapy session, interventions may be addressed to communicational processes, relationship interactions, and dynamic and genetic material, all of which are intimately connected.

Mate Choice

54   Since the main thrust of this book is with practical matters

concerning therapy, I shall say little more about mate choice. We can learn a great deal about this from the patients themselves, and I suggest that, whatever our theories may be, we pay careful attention to the versions they provide. In a majority of marriages, shared sociocultural, religious, and more personal values, standards, interests, and attitudes represent significant *conscious* elements in mate choice. These factors continue to operate as factors that hold people together in general, as well as in the marriage relationship. Despite the growing ecumenical movement, for example, a Roman Catholic is not likely to feel comfortable, or to remain long, at a Southern Baptist convention. If not too rigidly applied, the dictum that one should not select a mate too different in terms of religion, social and economic status, and so forth, is also psychologically sound.

Of more concern to the marriage therapist are those compelling forces, for the most part *outside* the couple's awareness, that operate cohesively or disruptively in the relationship. With his psychological insight, and from his more objective vantagepoint, the therapist is in a better position to tune in to these more important variables and to bring them to the attention of his patients.

Dyadic Vicious Circles

With couples who do not start out with serious communicational problems, the therapist can observe, even quite early in therapy, a specifically dyadic dynamism. A patient in individual therapy or in another form of marriage therapy would not be able to tell the therapist about it, because each member of the couple is completely unaware of what he or she is doing to the other or why they are unable to resolve certain relationship problems despite their earnest desire to do just that. Because it is fashionable just now, I suppose, 55 the patients usually say that they have trouble communicating; what they actually mean is that neither can get the other to meet his expectations. The harder they try, the more they fail. Often they are aware of a deep sense of hurt, frustration, irritation, or bitterness. Whatever affection, tenderness, or warmth they may have been capable of feeling earlier in their courtship or marriage has long since been eroded away. (I am speaking mainly of conflicted marriages, where couples have applied for therapy because of their distress about their relationship. The frustration and alienation, however, in the "normal" spouse responding to symptoms—hysteria, anxiety, phobias, depression—in the identified patient may produce a somewhat similar situation.) To explain this dynamism, let me set forth the procedure I use and have found effective in demonstrating to the couple the nature of their interaction:

Let's pretend we have a strip of movie film or videotape of the interaction between the two of you during the past ten minutes. Let's take four or five feet of it and splice it together so skillfully that you can't tell where the splice is. Also, suppose we imagine that we can select out and view each of your frames separately on a screen over there. I want to be perfectly fair, so I'll close my eyes and push one of the two buttons I have here in my desk—a John button and a Mary button.

Here is John's frame showing up first; the three of us will watch it together. We see John sitting there like a bump on a log puffing at his pipe, tuning himself out. He drags his heels; he refuses to do anything constructive. He gives weak excuses for his failure to act responsibly. We can't help thinking, "My God, what an inconsiderate, uncooperative bastard! He must be mighty difficult to live with: He'd drive any woman up a wall trying to get him to do anything at all. Probably their house is falling down all around them, and he won't lift a finger to help his poor harassed wife."

O.K. Now that you've had your turn, John, I'll push the Mary button. What's this we see now? We see a woman who nags and nags, and we hear her strident shrieking. Her voice sounds for all the world like a machine gun. We think, "What a terrible woman to have to listen to! She'd drive any man to distraction. A regular bitch on wheels! Her husband must wish he had a hearing aid he could turn off, or else that he could flee her presence to protect himself from her. He probably wouldn't do anything for her even if it were something he knew was good for both of them."

Then, addressing each in turn, I add:

The more you act the way you act, the more you act the way you act! Who's to blame? Nobody! There's no beginning and no end; it's a circle, a vicious circle. Each one pushes the other deeper into frozen, polarized positions without wanting to do it or being aware of doing it. For me to discern this pattern and to inform you of it is relatively easy. I've seen it so many times before. I must say, you have a lot of company. The tough part is getting it stopped. How are you going to get out of this painful squirrel cage you've been in for so many years?

I now settle back into the observer position and wait for their responses to my interpretation.

Dynamics, Genetics, and Transference Reactions

What did each patient bring with him in his individual personality that was conducive to the development of this pattern? With a question such as this, we move into a consideration of genetic, intrapsychic material. There are, of course, any number of pathways that lead to the same or similar end results, and there are several different ways of understanding those compelling unconscious forces that lead each individual to be vulnerable to participation in the kind of vicious circle just referred to. One of the spouses may have entered the relationship already overcompensating in the direction of cleanliness and orderliness to control the opposite tendencies in himself; very possibly he has been   57 reared in a "cleanliness-is-next-to-godliness" atmosphere. Let's assume that this spouse is the wife, for this is more often the case. An average, expectable degree of uncleanliness or disorderliness in the husband will arouse her anxiety and set into motion an increase of her defense of overcompensation. In order to decrease her own anxiety, she must pressure her husband to "shape up"; by doing this she has externalized her conflict. If the husband does, indeed, shape up, she will then no longer have to deal with her inner conflict. Unless other factors extraneous to the marital relationship force the issue, she will never have to deal with this inner problem and will remain a mildly compulsive housewife. She may appear and feel relatively "normal." On the other hand, let's assume that before he ever met his wife, the husband had been up to his eyebrows in parental overcontrol. His mother was strict, domineering, and inflexible with respect to the same or different content areas. The wife's efforts to maintain or restore her own balance may be relatively gentle but may impinge on the husband through what we may consider his "mother filter," in other words, through a negative transferential reaction. The husband overreacts, becomes angry, and expresses his anger either covertly or overtly in his verbal or other behavior. In the interview he may go into a pouting silence, or he may shout, "You and your goddamn house; you think more of it than you do of me." At home he may shout or "forget" to take his rubbers off and track mud across the recently cleaned and waxed foyer.

When these dynamisms are directly observed in interview behavior, the opportunity to interpret them is at hand. Accordingly, I tell the husband that he appears to be acting as if he has just received a direct order from a top sergeant, when, to me, it seemed that his wife had made a reasonable request or just expressed a wish. If he can recognize and acknowledge that he has distorted and overreacted, we are halfway to uncovering and interpreting the negative transferential aspects involved. I find that patients quickly and easily grasp the analogy of a distorting and amplifying filter (or persistent image) that has been set in place during the impressionable years of childhood. Another way of expressing this would be: "I get the impression that you sometimes, or many times, perceive your husband through your father filter; you don't see and hear him as he really is or the way he comes through to me."

Obviously, if the husband's transference reaction to his wife is resolved, only half the problem is solved. Indeed, much of the time his is not actually a transference reaction; his wife, driven by her anxiety, appears to him abrasively domineering. When I am reasonably sure that the irritation I sense is not a product of the distorting and amplifying effects of one of my own filters, I tell the patient that, although it was not directed specifically at me, what he is doing is irritating to me. I explain, further, that one of the ways I work is to place myself now in his place, now in his wife's, to find out what it feels like there. Then I return to my own seat to think and to respond.

The next step is to get at the wife's anxiety and driveness and to find out where these arise from *within her*. Often it comes from the same or a similar place as the husband's transference to his wife: inner commands out of the past. It may be the voice of father or mother speaking: "Pull down your dress and sit like a lady." "How many times have I told you to wash your hands before you sit down to dinner?" "Straighten up your room, you naughty girl, or no television tonight!" I am sure that my readers are well aware how frequently parental disciplinary practices are much harsher than the above examples, imparting a sense of profound badness and a need for a strict and binding confirmity, both self- and other-directed.

Therapist–patient transference–countertransference re-   59 actions have been extensively and intensively discussed by others, and I will purposefully refrain from considering them extensively. One phenomenon that occurs in a triadic relationship, and that may be typical of some triangles generally, occasionally occurs when I have come down particularly hard on one spouse. Then, the patients, who may not have agreed on anything yet in therapy, and only rarely elsewhere, form an alliance against me. This may be a first step in closing the gap or strengthening the bonds between them.

Adaptive Then, Maladaptive Now

Another common phenomenon—or perhaps another way of looking at, understanding, and interpreting behavior—is to regard a behavioral mode as a survival technique learned in one's family of origin; this behavioral mode has persisted into the present and, in these changed circumstances, has become maladaptive. How frustrating and dismaying to find that something that in the past always worked, even earned praise, now brings condemnation down upon one's head! Since the behavior involved is automatic (and unconscious), the patient is not able to think about it or to examine it. The husband who cannot tolerate feelings of tenderness, sentiment, warmth, or gentleness is a good example. We all know that, give the cultural pressure put on most boys in our society, it is difficult enough under the best of circumstances for men to get in touch with their own feelings or those of others: "Big boys don't cry!" In a job, profession, or career, this is an asset. To be able to think logically and to act decisively, feelings must be kept under control and relegated to a secondary position. But what about the man who is totally unable to shift gears and hence cannot relate to an emotionally needful wife and family when it is necessary and safe, and would be fulfilling for him, too, to do so?

Undoubtedly the atmosphere of such a man's family of origin was austere. As he observed and experienced it, the marriage relationship of his parents was sterile in terms of closeness and demonstrativeness. His parents may have been a good team; they may have worked well together, and their relationship may have seemed smooth and untroubled. Both may have been loving and accepting enough when their children were in the infant or toddler stage, but the parents may have had definite attitudes about the age when feelings in the children should be suppressed. This child soon learned that to get along with mother and father he had to hide his feelings—and he did. Soon such feelings became so obscured and repressed that they became quite inaccessible to him. Now that he is an adult, feelings of any tender sort, both in himself and in his family, produce profound anxiety in him, and he must defend himself against them.

How did this man come to select an emotionally warm wife who expects responsiveness in her mate? During their courtship he could both tolerate and express some romantic, tender feelings, at intervals and in small doses. On an unconscious level, his future wife was also tuning into the alien, but feeling, little boy in him. Furthermore, during the courtship and engagement periods such behavior is culturally expected. This he learned from movies and television. After the marriage and the honeymoon, both of their bubbles burst. The stage is now set for a progressively widening gap between them. The wife expects a deepening of intimacy and closeness, according to the marriage model she had experienced and the way she had been treated in the past. The husband, for his part, expects his marriage to unfold along the lines of his own marriage-model experience. Each accepts unconsciously that "what was good for mom and dad is good for us."

One way for the man to protect himself against his wife's expectations, which soon intensify into demands, is for him *61* to immerse himself in his business or profession. As he spends more and more of his time and energy at work, his behavior at home sinks deeper and deeper into withdrawal of exhaustion. Gradually the wife becomes more shrewish and sexually rejecting. At the same time she may seek satisfaction for her emotional hunger in an extramarital involvement. Their high hopes and reasonable expectations have turned into despair for both. They consult their clergyman, attorney, or family physician, who recommends marriage therapy. Depending on her individual history and dynamics, the wife may develop symptoms that serve to compel the husband to attend to her emotional needs. Furthermore, the wife's "sickness" may legitimize for the husband the expression of his feelings of caring. The husband—who has never been able to say, simply, "I love you," or bring his wife an inexpensive gift for no particular reason (that is, not on one of the many commercially devised occasions that almost compel him to do so)—may knock himself out showing that he cares about his phobic wife by relieving her of many of her responsibilities.

In these circumstances the task of the therapist is clear and can be accomplished through the tactics and strategies already discussed. In extreme cases, I sometimes tell the couple that in my opinion the question is not whether they are to be divorced. To all intents and purposes they already are divorced. The question now is whether they will be able to remarry. Put another way, divorces do not take place in courtrooms any more than marriages take place in churches; they occur between people. The courtroom scene of a divorce represents only the formalization of something that occurred long before.

Early in my experience with conjoint marital psychotherapy I was greatly surprised at how quickly each spouse could understand the dynamics of the other, when it was put to them in terms of learned adaptive strategies.

What I had failed to take into account was that each one already knew the explanations I was offering them. They lacked only the ability to apply to themselves what they already knew in a way that would permit growth away from and out of the rigid molds they were in, toward a new pattern that would be tolerable and gratifying to both. When I inquire, "Where do you suppose a man learns how to treat a woman?" the wife is, in general, able to answer accurately. With just a little more support she could spell out what it was like to be a little boy in her husband's family of origin, exactly what he learned and what he did not learn there. (She knows her husband's parents well, of course.) Making these connections and articulating them softens her defenses, bitterness, rejection, and symptoms, as well as his callousness and his withdrawal.

The husband can now be asked, "Where do you think a woman learns what to hope for or to expect from her man?" which leads to a similar alteration and modification of his understanding of her. As therapy progresses, the husband loosens up somewhat and can tolerate and express more of the feelings he has been repressing. There are still limitations to how loose he can become. A draft horse cannot be made into a race horse. The wife, accordingly, will have to scale down her hopes and expectations. It may be necessary for the therapist to help her find, outside the marriage, sources of gratification of her emotional needs that will not threaten the marital relationship.

Two other expectations mates commonly have about their spouses deserve mention. One, which operates outside of awareness, may be expressed as: If only I can pick a wife (husband) somewhat similar to my father (mother) and have it come out differently this time. He or she will meet those needs that bad father (mother) did not, when I was a child. What a triumph! All those hurts, disillusionments, and humiliations will be magically undone. This "reasoning" is   63 somewhat similar to what Edmund Bergler has called magic gestures. ("See world, this is the way bad mother (father) should have treated me.")

The other pattern, also unconscious, runs: "I shall choose a mate who is the negative (in a photographic sense) of my mother (father). Then everything will be completely different." The problem here is that one who chooses according to this romantic formula all too often widely overshoots the mark. A recent clinical example illustrates this. A woman whose father was lacking in intelligence, indolent, passive, and indecisive chose a husband she thought intelligent, ambitious, aggressive, and decisive. Her description of him matched my perceptions of him. Unfortunately, his aggression could take destructive forms when he was sufficiently provoked. On several occasions prior to therapy he had slapped, punched, or pushed her. Once during therapy he blackened one of her eyes. Although she filed for and later cancelled a divorce action, the woman gave herself away as she recounted the incident in which her husband had given her the black eye. Her eyes sparkled, and she had a difficult time controlling a joyful smile. This offered me the opportunity to confront her with her unverbal glee, which was very close to consciousness, and to get at the dynamics and genetics of this side of her.

Role Modeling and Role Playing

The male therapist responds feelingly to the wife when this is appropriate, serving as a new and different role model for the husband to identify with. If modeling and other therapeutic moves fail to soften the husband's defensiveness, however, the therapist may turn to role playing. I might say to the husband, "John, you be me, and I'll be you." I then invite the wife to involve herself with me. I purposefully respond to the wife in such a manner that the husband can directly observe the advantages to be gained from doing the same thing. The less intelligent and less sophisticated patients regularly require a concrete demonstration of this sort.

At this point the reader may be puzzled that I have mentioned sex only three times so far, once suggesting that it would be unwise to discuss it then. I regard sexual behavior as *not separate* from, or discontinuous with, other aspects of the marital relationship. In seven or eight out of ten cases, when the relationship in general improves, so does the specifically sexual part of it. In some instances, this occurs without the subject being discussed in depth and without specifically sexually oriented interpretations having been offered. However, sexual matters are important and complex enough to merit a chapter of their own.

CHAPTER IV

Sex in the Jungle:
The Middle Phase of Therapy
(CONTINUED)

*T*HE COUPLE sitting before me in my consultation room discussing the pros and cons of attending some particular movie are the same people who may, later that evening, undress and attempt to negotiate a sexual experience. When they shed their clothing, however, they do not by any means shed their personalities. Exceptional, indeed, are couples who are able to compartmentalize their sex lives, that is, to make something entirely separate of them. Almost invariably the bedroom scene is contaminated with feelings from today and yesterday and earlier—exhaustion, fear, worry, conflicts, humiliations, resentments, vindictiveness. Forbidding ghosts and distressing memories out of the recent or distant past crowd, with their interfering vibrations, in upon the two.   *67*

From the point of view of the marriage therapist, the wonder is not that human beings have difficulty in this highly charged and delicately balanced situation but that it is ever a complete success.

Added to all this is the tragic ignorance about sexuality that is so commonplace in our society today in both men and women, despite the fact that so much is talked and written about it. Only recently have the efforts of sex educators and the flood of informative books about sex begun to make a dent in our societal failure to properly inform children, teen-agers, and young adults about this crucially important area of their lives. The increased openness about sexual behavior all about us—in movies and popular magazines, on television and radio—has undoubtedly been helpful to those suffering from blockings and inhibitions in their sex lives. I heartily dislike the expression "sexual inadequacy," because it is not psychologically accurate. However, information and attitudes acquired later in life are weak medicine with which to combat values, feelings of guilt, shame, anxiety, and misinformation that were acquired early. It should also be noted that most of the films rated X still maintain a Victorian flavor: In the end, something bad happens to those who have been shown enjoying their sexual appetites.

Information and interpretations imparted verbally by a trusted authority figure are influences much more powerful than books or articles that are recommended to children or patients. When a parent, without comment, hands a child or teen-ager a book to read, the second and unspoken part of the message is quite clear to the youngster: "Here, read for yourself about this unspeakable thing." I do not, of course, give my patients "birds and bees" lectures, although I do consider part of my function to be educational. What I do is to fill in informational gaps and, when necessary, correct misapprehensions.

The Menstrual Cycle:
Its Effect on Women and Their Mates

Interpretations of psychopathological reactions—dynamic and genetic—associated with menstruation constitute an integral part of marriage therapy. For the most part, men do not have the foggiest notion about the profound effect that menstruation has upon their wives. It comes to them as an empathy-inducing revelation to learn of the humiliation, shame, embarrassment, fear, and even feelings of dirty inferiority that their wives experienced at the onset of their menses. Even more important, both spouses learn that these long-forgotten feelings still powerfully influence the wife's state of mind and emotional balance when menstruation is impending or occurring. The biological fact of being female is only a part of the story. Society and the particular culture play their part as well. I often find myself weaving together the sociocultural and biological threads in an explanation like the following:

Hold it a minute, John. You're reacting pretty strongly to your wife's being upset at your forthcoming business trip. Let me try to help you understand by explaining why I think she's reacting the way she is. From the time Mary was about so high (indicating), it seemed to her as though girls were always getting the short end of the stick. It is almost certain that her parents kept the reins pulled much tighter on her than they did on her brothers. The boys were encouraged to go out and climb trees, to explore the world, as it were, while she was kept at home and enjoined to behave like a proper young lady. Then, when she started to menstruate, she was both shocked and frightened at first, if no one gave her the proper explanation; for a while she may even have feared she was bleeding to death. After her periods started, her parents probably watched over her even more closely, at the very time her brothers were being given more freedom. How else could she have felt but resentful and envious? Right now she is beginning

69

her period, and you're about to leave tomorrow for a business trip. Sure, you know that traveling is, or at least can be, pretty uncomfortable and that you'll be working—and working hard—most of the time. But all of Mary's old feelings are being stirred up anew. To her it's the way it used to be when she was the sister who had to stay home. You're the brother who had all the freedom, going off now to romantic San Francisco, to see the world.

I have found that both spouses profit from this kind of explanation, since both are now in a position to better understand the wife's present overreaction to the husband's (necessary) business trip. He will be more tolerant of her distress, however it may be expressed; and she will be better able to accept his leaving. Some airline, as well as the wife, may even profit later when the husband goes out of his way to arrange some trip so that his wife can accompany him. Or at the very least, out of his newfound understanding, he may arrange for some kind of compensation or reward for her.

When we stop to think of the general reaction to the whole matter of menstruation, it is an interesting and deplorable, although little-known, fact that, in the English language, no word exists with *positive* connotations to denote menstruation. There are, to be sure, the neutral "menstruation," or "period," or "Today I had a visitor." There are certainly negative words: "curse", or "being unwell", or "coming sick." To help both spouses to better understand the wife's negative feelings about herself and her menstrual periods, I make a point of asking them if they know any way of talking about menstruation that suggests it is something of worth or pride. Almost universally I find that they get the message and come to realize how our very language helps to mold and limit our feelings and our attitudes. Lately I have experimented with formulating and suggesting positive language, for example, "My flower is in full bloom." Thus, I was very interested when a husband not long ago offered, "My days of renewal are near," This innovative tactic is proving felicitous.

At this point one might logically examine words that refer specifically to male sexuality: "erection," "potency," "hard-on." Yet, for the man, these concepts constitute a double-edged sword. When things go well, he can feel proud and powerful; but it is also possible for him to feel humiliated and without worth when he is not erect, when he is impotent or soft.

Under "normal" circumstances in which the woman has only minimal conflicts concerning her femaleness, there are, without doubt, psychological concomitants to the biological phases of the menstrual cycle. During the last third of the cycle, when the possibility of pregnancy is anticipated, some of the woman's energy turns inward. Psychologically she is preparing herself for pregnancy, whether pregnancy is consciously desired or not. This energy is, in some measure, withdrawn from her husband, and during this time the wife's interest in sexual activity diminishes. Depending on his sensitivity, the husband may experience this as depriving and rejecting of him, which it undoubtedly is from his point of view, or he may take it personally, as a reflection on him. Thus, the stage is set, month after month, for some kind of friction to occur between the couple. Where profound fear of pregnancy exists, similar dynamics come into play. When the therapist apprehends either pattern coming to light during the interview, it is time for an explanation that can and should be reassuring to both.

Male nonphysician readers (unless they have been educated through experiences with their mates) may be unaware of a common physiological phenomenon that coincides with the last third of the menstrual cycle, that is beginning about ten days before the first day of the period. Due to salt retention, fluid collects in the woman's body, and her tissues become waterlogged. Tensions and irritability 71 arise as a consequence of this uncomfortable, though benign, physical problem. Medical treatment in the form of a low-salt diet or a mild diuretic regularly solves this difficulty, and informing the husband about the problem is helpful to him and, in turn, to the wife as well.

Parenthood

Becoming a parent, when it is a reasoned, agreed-on choice accompanied with appropriate, positively tinged feelings and when both spouses possess enough psychic energy to make emotional room for another, is an enriching experience. A couple deprived by nature of such an opportunity often need therapy to come to terms with this circumstance, to prevent its leading to an ever widening rift between the spouses. The one whose anatomy or physiology is "at fault" may desperately need the compassionate support of the other. At the same time, the spouse's hurt and disappointment may make it impossible for him or her to give such support. Adoption of a child is not a solution unless and until these feelings are worked through and the couple are at peace concerning the matter—at peace with themselves and with each other. Conjoint marital psychotherapy offers the couple the opportunity to receive emotional support from the therapist while they confront the issues and feelings involved.

My own experience with the problems of adoptive parents and their children has been too limited for me to speak authoritatively about this much-neglected topic. Those few who have consulted me were the parents of children already in their late adolescence who were in profound turmoil and conflict about their identity. My impression is that the parents would have needed therapy prior to adoption, during the early months after receiving their infant, and at intervals thereafter, first as a preventive measure and then at the first sign of trouble.

I can look back on considerable experience treating couples with infants and toddlers and on some work with couples experiencing pregnancy. When pregnancy ensues, and especially during the third trimester, the wife tends to become more and more a mother and less and less a wife. She is caught up, emotionally and in her fantasy, in the awesome and glorious mystery unfolding within her body. (I am referring to pregnancies that are minimally conflicted.) While the mother-to-be prepares herself psychologically for the necessary symbiotic relationship with her infant, the husband is apt to be shocked and thrown off balance by his wife's unexpected and, to him, inexplicable withdrawal. His qualitative and quantitative reaction will be determined by his past experiences in his family of origin and his dynamcics, Actually, in marriage pregnancy and childbirth are two of the most commonly encountered precipitating events for the onset of symptoms or symptomatic behavior in either spouse or for the onset of marital difficulty. While, under the best of circumstances, knowing what to expect may prove to be a slender reed for some couples, it does help others to cope with the crisis better than they could have without such knowledge. For the therapist to explain the average dynamics of motherhood, even several years after the fact, has proved helpful. Turning the coin over and explaining the husband's reaction to his wife's unexpected feelings and behavior has also been beneficial. Each spouse can gain insight into those emotional factors that, in the past, set their troubles in motion. Obviously, the more fragile their marital rapport before pregnancy and childbirth, the more profound will be the ensuing difficulties and the more difficult the therapy. We know that in an overloaded circuit plugging in one more appliance blows the fuse. That is the kind of language I use to explain to the couple what happened to them. This marital history material can be profitably considered only after the higher-priority problems have been at least partially resolved—here again, the problem of process versus content confronts us.

New Marital Relationships

During the past five to ten years, increasing numbers of couples have established quasi-marital relationships. Openly and honestly, they discuss the limits of their currently existing emotional commitment to each other. Before engaging fully in sexual intercourse, as they would in a marriage, they explore their feelings about it with each other, in an effort to determine what they can live with. Usually they decide to go ahead with a sexual relationship, and usually the young woman goes on the pill. At the other extreme of this particular continuum are those couples who have discussed neither where they are with each other nor how far they intend to go with each other sexually. One thing leads inevitably and expectably to another: pregnancy; a hurried marriage fraught with all manner of trauma, weeping, and wailing; a confession scene to both sets of parents; blaming and accusing, with, finally, at least one of the mothers, fathers, or grandparents refusing to attend the wedding.

Obviously, other things being equal, the arrangement first described above is the less hazardous of the two, at least on the face of it, My experience with both patterns has definitely confirmed this. Even though the first couple have been as careful as wisdom and experience allowed, they may later be overtaken by unexpected guilt. The second pair, burdened with the myth that "we *only* (or mainly) married because . . .," all too often, in spite of therapy, continue to mindlessly fall into one disaster after another. In their
74 relationship, they have virtually nothing to go back to,

nothing to build upon. For them, if a relationship is to be formed, it must be built from scratch, after marriage or in therapy. I realize, of course, that many shades of grey emerge between the all-black, all-white circumstances as I have described them.

Actually, the extreme case has been nonexistent in my patient sample. The "only because . . ." myth does exist, yet the therapist must not permit himself to be deluded by the patients' retrospective reconstruction and their report to him that this was, indeed, the case. He must find out *why* they came together in that particular fashion, and impart these understandings to the couple. The following dynamics are frequently encountered:

1. Because of excessive dependency and low self-esteem, the young woman submits to the pressure put on her (however gentle and tentative it may be), convinced that the only way she can hold the man is by having intercourse with him.

2. Driven by fear concerning his masculinity, the man acts in a pseudoaggressive manner, and the woman, equally fearful about her femininity, succumbs.

3. Both are so guilt-ridden that neither can take the responsibility for reaching the sexual endpoint. In collusion and unaware, they rationalize that their sexual encounter was caused by being overwhelmed by a moment of passion, perhaps while under the influence of a drink too many.

4. Both are so indecisive, perhaps out of fear of making a mistake, that they must leave it to fate to catapult them into a marriage that both of them really (on some level) need and want.

5. Out of their mistrust of object relationships, neither is able to make a clear, openly articulated, emotional commitment to any other human being. Thus each must fall back on the "we had to because . . ." rationalization.

6. They may have been acting in a sexually free manner that was only skin deep and were unsophisticated about the use of contraceptives or encountered a genuine contraceptive failure. It must be pointed out, however, that such pseudofreedom can also occur with those who, at the beginning, were able to talk it through.

When the therapist is able to bring these usually interdigitating defensive maneuvers out into the open, together with the past experiences that made such maneuvers necessary, the couple have an opportunity to find other, more fulfilling, reasons for staying together than the myth with which they began.

Much has been written about the subject of contraception. Suffice it to say here that every marriage therapist should inform himself fully on the subject. He should not be surprised by the patient's genuine astonishment when he (the therapist) challenges the conviction that the pregnancy was an "accident." I confidently expect varying degrees of dismay, at first, when I inquire, "Well, how do you now understand that the pregnancy came about?"

Specific Forms of Common Sexual Constraints —Indirect Therapeutic Techniques

Trouble with the physical aspects of love-making is often a chief complaint. Many patients report and believe it is their only problem, but I rarely found that it occurs in pure form.

Making love is a special way of being together emotionally and of communicating verbally and nonverbally. How the couple act in these respects in the therapist's office accurately reflects the special way that they are together and communicate sexually. It should come as no surprise, then, that couples that function mainly on the level of blaming or of attack–counterattack, or who are generally burdened by guilt, either do not come together sexually at all, or, if they do, that some kind of disaster should occur. It is quite understandable that couples caught in dyadic vicious circles are not able to call a temporary truce and enjoy each other's bodies. Between them, only the content of the transaction changes. Why should we be surprised, in the case of a bossy husband who treats his wife like a rebellious teen-ager, while she acts like one, that the wife reacts to his order for sex in the same way that she reacts to any other order of his? As one patient aptly put it, "When he acts like a Hitler in the living room, I can't treat him like Maurice Chevalier in the bedroom." When the therapist successfully treats the vicious circle, disregarding its specific content but pointing out the process from which it has resulted, and assists the couple to replace it with something more benign, the couple will take that something with them into the bedroom.

Blatant refusal of either spouse to participate in sexual activity is easily handled therapeutically and does not require special consideration. The psychological short-circuiting into impotence, premature ejaculation, or frigidity has not occurred and does not require translation back into relationship terms before dealing with sexual activity.

Frequently, the marriage therapist is confronted by a teaming up of an impotent man, fearful of appropriate assertiveness on his part for any number of underlying reasons, and a woman afraid of healthy male aggressiveness. Such couples often wait to enter therapy until several years of frustration have passed. While both may have consciously desired sexual fulfillment their delay in seeking therapy can be regarded as a measure of their unconscious tendencies in the opposite direction. During the course of their therapy, the therapist may actually witness the man beginning to become erect verbally and nonverbally—in his voice tone, his body posture, the tensing of his skeletal musculature. 77

At the same time the wife may become increasingly anxious or act in such a way as to put a stop to her husband's erection, despite the fact that this is precisely what she has said she desires. The husband then regularly loses his (nonsexual) erection. I no longer wait until I have observed this pattern several times before I move in on it therapeutically. Once the husband is able to maintain his erection in the therapy setting, and the wife, overcoming her fear and defensiveness, can tolerate and begin to enjoy it, a resolution of the explicitly sexual problem will shortly follow.

Men who consciously seek sexual responsiveness in their wives, but who unconsciously abhor it—because of various motivations and attitudes of guilt, shame, or feelings that in sex "nice" is equivalent to "unsexy" and "not nice" to "sexy"—often enter into a sexually sterile tandem with a so-called frigid wife. It is not uncommon for such wives—at least those who get away with it within themselves—to be quite sexually responsive in a clandestine setting with some other man or a boyfriend. In the interview, for example, the therapist may observe the wife literally or figuratively raising her skirts to reveal her potential sexual responsiveness, possibly without overt sexual expression, ever so slightly. In some manner the husband may stop his wife from going further, by a disapproving facial expression, for example. The therapist then attacks this surface behavior in an effort to help the couple understand the hidden dynamics behind this interaction.

More Direct Therapeutic Tactics

Direct therapeutic approaches to sexual constraints are usually indicated later rather than earlier in therapy. Those cases in which sexual material begins and remains the central focus of the therapy are exceptional. I cannot overemphasize

78

the importance of the therapist's being clearly and deeply aware of his own feelings, attitudes, and values in this area. It is crucial for the therapist to confront sexual issues directly, openly, and sometimes even bluntly. If a patient advocates more sexual freedom while at the same time continuing to sound Victorian or prudish, this must be brought to his attention as well as to his spouse's. Obviously a therapist who is overly delicate or perhaps even constricted might, for his own comfort, let this pass. He might permit his couple to talk around the edges of their sexualtiy, avoiding such statements as: "Well, it's no surprise to me that you have trouble doing what you can't talk about except by pussyfooting around." This sort of comment should not be suppressed.

Use of Wit and Humor

I have found that the use of wit and humor, including at times apt cartoons or even sexually tinged stories (must we call them "dirty" or "off-color"?) very useful in helping couples loosen up on their antisex attitudes and inhibitions. These can be effective in other content areas as well: I often describe a cartoon I saw some years ago, probably in *The New Yorker*, in which two caveman are standing at the entrance of a cave, gesticulating and looking off into the jungle. Inside two cavewomen are looking at the tastefully decorated cave, obviously belonging to one of the couples. The caption reads: "Did you do it yourself, or did you have a decorator?" Most people require a concrete elaboration of the intense symbolic importance to most women of the home and the relatively lesser importance that most men attach to it.

A sexually tinged cartoon that I sometimes bring in when the couple is sedulously avoiding any risk in putting into practice what they have learned in therapy depicts a couple in bed. The man is reading, while the unhappy-looking, voluptuous spouse lies there with her arms folded. The caption reads, "Be patient, darling, just one more visit to the psychiatrist." To those who feel compelled to mechanically schedule their lives, generally as well as sexually ("Let's plan for sex every Friday night") I like to tell the following story:

A couple with a fertility problem put themselves through arduous chores of temperature taking and graphing in order that their sexual relations coincide as precisely as possible with ovulation, even though they were severely limiting their enjoyment. They follow this structured procedure for months without success and, greatly disappointed, return to their physician for further advice. He now changes the plan around completely and instructs them to be completely spontaneous, having relations whenever and wherever the spirit moves them. This works. The wife soon becomes pregnant, and they have a lovely baby. But there is a complication: They have been banned from the United Nations Building for the rest of their lives.

There are other ways of introducing an element of earthy humor into therapy. With inhibited, guilt-ridden patients I have sometimes said, in a tone of mock seriousness, "I'd like to give you two a prescription to replace those sleeping pills you both indulge in. A hot meat injection, as needed, is a much better sedative than any pill I know about, and much more fun, too." My aim is to be free enough, myself, that I can be a littlely "naughty" and thereby slightly loosen up their overly rigid consciences.

A few warnings about the use of humor, however, are in order. The therapist must be sure that his wit does not arise from rancor toward his patients and that it represents a genuine laughing together about shared human problems and experiences. I prefer to frame my more confronting and unpalatable comments or interpretations in such terms as, "We all share . . ." or "Most of us human beings. . . " For the therapist to be able to gauge how far he can go with which couple is also critically important—a few inches beyond where they are, but not far enough to shock or offend them, is desirable.

Letting matters rest at a humorous level can also be hazardous: It could lead to a later increase in guilt and, thus, backfire. I almost always follow up humor with a serious comment about the couple's plight. In the case of the mock serious prescription I might add, depending on circumstances: "I have been joking a bit with you, but I also mean all this very seriously; the two of you have been depriving yourselves of possibilities of pleasure and relaxation that you both richly deserve."

Whether we like it or whether we approve, the double standard and sterotypic expectations of role models are still with us. Therefore, the use of certain kinds of humor and language may not, even now, be open to female or clerical therapists. Each individual must determine whether the use of humor fits his and the couple's personality.

I have also found certain other techniques effective in more direct treatment of sexual constraints: Without going into details, these are to:

1. Suggest—only after we have together considered sexual matters in some depth—that patients read selected books combining sexuality with beauty and warmth. (See "Suggested Readings for Patients.")

2. Instruct the couple to call a moratorium on attempting to have complete sexual relations; that is, either one is free to halt the proceedings as soon as he feels any discomfort. This will give us, at the next session, an opportunity to explore and understand the source of the trouble.

3. Advise the couple to get out of the rut, responsibilities, and pressures of their everyday lives by taking more frequent,

long-week-end type vacations (minihoneymoons, they might be called) *without the children,* either in place of, or in addition to, the usual "two-week" vacation per year.

One technique that may be unique with me, has proved to be most revealing and empathy enhancing:

Let's assume that we write down everything that goes into your love-making from beginning to end, like a menu card at a restaurant. Included would be such items as before-dinner drink, the appetizer, the soup, the salad, the entree, dessert, beverage, after-dinner drink. Now from this love-making menu of yours, I would like each of you to write down three and only three items that you would prefer this particular night. At another time you might select more or different things. Put your name at the top of the card and write down your choices.

After they have completed this part of the task, I continue, "Turn the card over and write down what you guess your spouse has just written. Then give the cards to me."

Sex and love-making are really labels. As such they are a form of shorthand that at one and the same time says too much and too little. The word "sex" covers a multitude of needs and desires that are felt but that the couple may never have shared. This fanciful exercise, and the discussion that follows, provides the opportunity. We quickly get down to specifics—understandings and misunderstandings, need consonances and need dissonances. It is an excellent way to clarify what has, up to this point, been dark and murky. Wives have commonly completely missed the importance of closeness to their husbands (who never put into words that they needed it), and husbands have missed the importance to their wives of penetration (since they never signaled their enjoyment of it). Many more examples can be cited.

From this chapter, the reader might conclude that I make no use of the more traditional modes of interpretation in my therapeutic work. This is by no means the case! I make abundant use of psychoanalytic formulations and interpretations whenever the opportunity to do so arises out of the material. The reader can learn about these various concepts and their use in psychotherapy from many other sources— psychoanalytic and psychodynamic. Let me emphasize the importance I attach to understanding these concepts and techniques and to their use in the practice of conjoint marital therapy. Since it fits neither my conceptual framework nor my personality, I definately avoid mechanical methods in the treatment of sexual problems.

With those couples whose value system is violated by extramarital involvements (and these are in the majority in my patient sample), a spouse being "caught" in an affair is often the immediate precipitating event that brings the couple to therapy. The history and the course of their therapy, almost without exception, reveal that the marital relationship had been in serious disarray long before this straw-that-broke-the-camel's back incident took place. Because it represents only a species of symptomatic behavior, treatment unfolds along the same lines and does not call for additional consideration.

In a few cases I have identified what seemed to me to be benign or even therapeutic affairs, for example, in an otherwise solid marriage marred only by the couple's inability to overcome specifically sexual inhibitions due to mutual guilt and shame. The following clincial vignette is a good illustration:

A young physician and his wife had what could only be described as sterile and perfunctory sexual relations during their five years of married life. A few weeks before beginning therapy the husband was "turned on" by a sexy and passionate nurse at the hospital where he was serving his residency. Though younger than he, she was considerably more sexually experienced; not only did she   *83* teach him many things he didn't know, she also helped loosen up his overly strict conscience. He arranged to be "caught" by his wife, and she, in turn, had a "what's good for the goose is good for the gander" affair of her own. Actually, she had, before learning of her husband's experience, been stimulated by a fellow student at the university she was then attending. This young man helped her as the young nurse had helped her husband. Their conjoint marital therapy was brief and successful; they needed to be helped to understand what had happened and why and to work through their hurt and dismay at not doing for each other what their respective paramours had done

CHAPTER V

The End of The Safari:
Terminal Phase of Therapy

*N*O SHARP delineation marks off one phase of therapy from another; rather, one phase shades gradually into the next. I have, however, come to recognize certain signs as indicative of the ending phase of therapy. First, I am more relaxed and quiet and less impelled to act. Thus, I remain in the observer role for longer periods of time and feel more confident in the patients' own ability to use the tools they have learned during the earlier phases of therapy. The couple, too, seem less tense. Their arguments contain less heat and more light. Issues are resolved and plans made, even carried out. There is considerably less contradicting of each other with regard to events that took place between sessions. Negative goals of a dispute—for example, fixing blame—have been replaced with more positive goals, such as learning how each contributed to some misunderstanding. More sentences begin with "I" instead of with "you." Those that do begin with "you" are more often oriented toward understanding, searching for, or suggesting how the other may feel or have felt. (To certain couples, I would already have pointed out in earlier stages of therapy their tendency to begin every sentence, or most of them with "you"—the "mote-in-the-other guy's-eye" position.)

Again, Content versus Process

At this stage I deal more with content than with process. In effect, the therapy becomes more analytic. During interview segments, sometimes even during an entire session, one spouse is definitely in the "patient" position, with the other observing or joining in as a co-therapist might. While in earlier phases this sort of one-to-one response would have obscured communicational and relationship problems, it now proves effective. Transferences that either patient has developed toward the therapist surface and require attention, although they may appear at any time, even in the first evaluation interview, and must, of course, be handled then and there. The transferences may be analyzed in the more usual sense or reversed through the use of corrective emotional experiences.

By "corrective emotional experiences" I mean that the therapist does not correspond to the patient's idiosyncratic anticipations as to how a person—one who is in authority and upon whom the patient is somewhat dependent—will act. For example, a patient who has been reared with the stringently enforced caveat that one must respect his elders, never question their opinions, and never, never talk back, summons up the courage to gently disagree with the therapist. I answer, "You may be right about that. In any event,

86

I like your challenging me in this way better than your just taking everything I say on faith, as you've been doing up to now." Or a man who has been put down as a child for showing any kind of tender ("weak") feelings now dares to respond to his wife's pain with a little tenderness. At this point I say, "Congratulations! That was a real breakthrough and took a lot of guts." Then I ask the spouse how her husband's move affected her feelings. Earlier in therapy, before the wife's defenses had softened, this might have been dangerous. Here, however, I have yet to receive an aversive reaction from a wife to her husband's attempt to reality-test a small display of tenderness. I do recall a dramatic example of a husband "breaking down" before his wife was ready or felt safe enough to join him. Our cocker spaniel, O'Malley, is my sometime "co-therapist." He offers a diversion for the patients from the serious business of therapy and serves to soften and humanize whatever remains of a clinical atmosphere in my consulting room. I was surprised one day when a husband wept genuine tears of sadness that his wife could not believe how much he cared for her. I did not then expect him to get in touch with and express these feelings. While the wife sat in stony silence, O'Malley jumped up on the couch and licked the husband's face. He responded automatically by hugging O'Malley. To the wife I said, "My God! Look what the dog did and how John reacted. I expect that John would have welcomed similar comforting from you, had you been able to provide it. Too bad you weren't. We'll need to understand that."

Transference Material

Generally, in conjoint marital psychotherapy, patient –therapist transference reactions are less intense than they are in analytically oriented individual psychotherapy: The

couple are heavily transferred to each other, and the transferences to the therapist are, therefore, diluted. In this form
of therapy, regression is kept to a minimum by focusing
on problem solving in the here-and-now, using the past
mainly for understanding the present, and conducting
therapy sessions at intervals of one week. (On occasion, when
the going is particularly rough, a couple may be granted
an extra interview.) For these reasons, I believe the terminal
phase in conjoint marital psychotherapy is less complicated
than in some other forms.

With some patients I use the more traditional,
analytic–interpretive approach, for instance, stating, "I have
the impression that, for reasons that are as yet unclear to
me, you are unwittingly trying to provoke me to anger."
If this hits the mark, we are in a position to explore the
unconscious purpose and meaning of the specific transference involved. In other cases I prefer to be more concrete,
open about my feelings, and dramatic. I might say,

"I'm quite irritated with you right now; let me explain why:
If I were an electrician whom you asked to examine what's wrong
with the wiring of your house, and he told you that your fuses
were blowing out because you had too many appliances in a circuit,
you'd probably follow his advice. I've made several explanations
about how things look to me, and each time you went right ahead
as if you hadn't heard me or weren't ready to give the slightest
thought to my ideas. That's why I'm irritated right now. Do you
have any idea what leads you to treat me like that?"

This suggests another path that can lead us to transference
reactions. Because the more concrete, open, and dramatic
approach has proven, in my work, to be more incisive and
efficient than the more traditional, analytic one, I now am
more inclined to use the former.

It often comes as a constructive revelation to the listening
88   spouse that I am having the same sort of difficulty with

his or her mate that she or he has been having. The husband, for instance, in the example above where the wife has ignored my suggestions, realizes that it's not a personal matter; his wife does not regard him as a stupid dope, as he had previously felt she did. Because of compelling events in her distant past, the wife has good reasons to mistrust the statements or suggestions of *any* male authority figure. My more open, honest, direct, and less defensive way of dealing with the circumstance also sets an example that can serve them well in the future. Instead of disengaging himself and fleeing more and more to the golf course, the husband is now able to stand his ground and work things out with his wife. Her understanding of the genesis of her transference reaction also helps her to listen better and to pay more attention to her husband's ideas.

The patient–therapist transference material is both more intense and more frequent later in therapy than it is earlier. This is a result, I suppose, of appearing as a blank screen more of the time; I more easily become a target for displacements and projections. This is not to say, however, that patient–therapist transferences occur more frequently or predominantly than spouse–spouse transferences. The latter continue to require most of the therapeutic work; the balance may shift to a 75–25 ratio, but, in my experience, no more than that.

The Use of Self-Revelation in Therapy

There are times and places throughout therapy where various degrees of self-revelation are useful. Opportunities to use this particular therapeutic tool arise more often in the later stages of therapy than in the earlier ones. Sometimes it is more efficacious to be the relatively blank screen, but there are also moments when the therapist may profitably   *89* reveal himself as the human being he is. I have learned to trust my feelings in such matters; the experienced therapist will do the same.

The following story shows that I, too, am a member of the club. I usually relate it when my patients are struggling to put into practice what they have learned in therapy and are hard on themselves for falling back into former patterns.

Early in our marriage, I found myself in a rage at my wife from time to time. After I calmed down and was able to think about it, I realized that my anger was obviously an overreaction. Although I had spent four years in analytic therapy, it took me months to figure out precisely what was happening. My rage was triggered whenever my wife suggested that I consider doing differently some project I had planned or that I was in the process of carrying out. Often her way was actually better, and had I listened to her at the start, instead of getting mad, I would have saved myself a lot of trouble. After thinking about this for a long time and examining my dreams and so forth for several weeks, what should have been obvious suddenly struck me. As a child I was close to and very much under the domination of a grandmother whom I experienced as extremely arbitrary and domineering. Whatever was to be done had to be done *her way* and no other. So it appeared to me then. Her power, authority, and influence seemed overwhelming. When my wife made a suggestion, however gently and tactfully, she pushed my "grandmother button." She did not know it, and I did not know it either. It took me several more months of strenuous work, with my wife's help, to begin to modify this reaction. Even now I am not completely free from this vulnerability, although I can truthfully say that it is under reasonably good control.

A less revealing, less detailed way to offer the same kind of reassurance is to state, with a bit of humor: "When you people become so perfect that you never become embroiled in any sort of snarl with each other, you just come back here to me, and I'll pay you the same fee I'm charging you to teach *me* how to do it! There's a limit to how good we humans can ever become. Anyway, a good fight now and then can clear the air and provide opportunity for further understanding and growth."

Experience indicates that my willingness to share vignettes from my personal life, my feelings, and attitudes does four things: It warms and humanizes the therapeutic atmosphere; it provides ego support; it lessens superego pressures; and, at the proper time, it fosters a more egalitarian "we're-all-in-this-together" state of mind, which I like. Most of my patients seem to like it, too, and to benefit from it.

Termination Proper

When spouses agree about ending or interrupting therapy I do not necessarily regard it as a resistance. As with other important decisions in their lives, I consistently take the position that this decision is theirs and theirs alone. This does not inhibit me from stating my view, judgment, or appraisal of their decision, once I have explored how they arrived at it, their feelings, motivations, and their possible negative transferences. If I consider their decision premature I say so, giving my reasons and my predictions as to the consequences. However I temper this by saying,

I hope that your judgment is sound and that mine is inaccurate. There's nothing much lost if your discontinuance should prove to be premature; you are free to call me and resume therapy if and when you feel the need. I may not be able to get to you immediately, but you can rest assured that you will have seniority over any new patients who may be on the waiting list.

Nor do I feel inhibited about raising the question of   91

whether the patients may be hanging on to treatment too long out of dependency, underestimation of their own strengths, a striving for an unrealistic perfection, or whatever I suspect may be blocking them from making this move. In conjoint marital psychotherapy I find that only a small minority of patients remain in therapy longer than I judge necessary. About 20 percent break off prematurely and return later for more therapy. My impression, in retrospect, is that although these terminations did prove to be premature, they filled a need at the time. The patients had to find things out for themselves, to experience an increase in their anxiety levels, and to renew their motivations.

About 5 percent of my patients do not actually become involved in therapy. They go through the evaluation interviews, attend one to four therapy sessions, and then drop out. In most of these cases the couple were not genuinely motivated to begin with, or else only one of them was. Usually the pair came under pressure of other interested parties (relatives, clergymen, physicians, attorneys) or as a peace offering to their consciences. They felt they had to give lip service to an attempt at therapy so that they could end with the feeling and the credentials of "We tried everything and nothing worked." They then do what they had already decided to do in the first place, although they may be unaware of this. Some patients are satisfied and terminate once their communicational problems have been clarified and resolved, some after these and their interactional ones have cleared. A majority of patients continue through all three stages of therapy and terminate only after they are satisfied with the depth of their dynamic and genetic understanding of themselves and of each other and their ability to use, on their own, the tools they have learned to work with in the therapy process. They depart hopeful about their potential for future growth.

At the time of termination three distinctly different circumstances may obtain:

1. The couple believe that they are sufficiently improved and that they can use successfully the tools they have learned to work with.

2. They believe that they are not improved, or only to a minimal degree, but that their situation has been clarified. They have come to terms with their inability for further growth; and they have decided, for any number of reasons, to remain together.

3. They have come to the conclusion, having worked diligently for change through therapy, that for them no change is possible and that the degree of their continuing pain now requires separation or divorce.

There are cases, of course, where only one of the spouses reaches the third position and the other must come to terms with this decision, if the other remains adamant about it. My records disclose that the third outcome has occurred regardless of what the specific presenting problem may have been, but it is exceedingly rare when one spouse in a viable marriage has sought therapy for a nonmarital problem, for example, a neurotic symptom such as headaches.

If the couples who terminate at the second position have not already learned that their decision to stay together arises from multiple motivations, I make a concerted effort to get this across to them, especially when they use the rationalization that it is "for the sake of the children." The realization that motivations are multiple is particularly crucial for the children, who should not bear the burden of their parents' martyrdom. I consider it an important function of the therapist to help the parents convey to their children that the parents are remaining together to meet *their own needs*.

The Terminal Interview

Once the couple have decided on termination, I begin the terminal interview by informing them that I would like to save some time "for review and feedback." Usually I allow twenty-five minutes or so for this task, longer, if the couple do not have much on their agenda. In asking them for a review I may say "I would like each of you to try to get in touch with and tell me of two or three things that have been meaningful and helpful to you, things that we have learned together either about yourself, each other, or your relationship." Obviously such a question can be raised only if it is clear that they have indeed made some degree of progress. For those who have not, some kind of reassurance that something may gell for them later or, perhaps, just congratulating them for having worked diligently at therapy may be helpful as parting comments. While some patients improve without developing insight in the classical sense, most do gain a better understanding of themselves, their spouses, and of the nature of their relationship. This is, of course, more often the case for those who have continued therapy through all three phases. It would not be true, for instance, for those who terminated once their communicational problems were resolved or somewhat improved. My purpose in asking for a review is twofold. I like to find out what *they* regard as having been significant, at least on a conscious level, rather than taking it for granted that *I* know what has been meaningful to the couple. I believe also that the lively discussion that ensues when I invite them to search their memories for this material reenforces, and emphasizes, and underlines what they have learned.

By asking for feedback I want a critique by the patients of my behavior throughout the therapy. I ask, "I would very much welcome your telling me what you can remember about

94

the things that I did that were helpful and, more importantly, the things that I did that were not helpful or that seemed downright harmful—things you liked and things you didn't like." This gives the couple an opportunity to ventilate any leftover feelings they have not been able to voice spontaneously. The answers to this question are informative to me as well. I learn some pleasant and some unpleasant things about how I have come through to them. And I do not dismiss these critical comments as representing transference only. During the therapy I have been quite visible to the couple as the human being I am. When I am convinced that what I am being told is transference, I try to deal with it on that level. If it clearly is not transference material, I own up to my shortcomings or simply listen. It may be necessary to deny too much credit for the results, when these have been reasonably good. I frequently find myself saying, "If you have learned from me, that says more about your ability to learn than about mine to teach; you are not giving yourselves enough of the credit." I have the very definite impression that this exercise is helpful to all of us and is sometimes even fun. Turning the tables seems a good note on which to end.

Therapy for Those Divorcing

Once the decision to divorce has been made, therapy usually continues for only a short time, perhaps two to five more sessions. At this point—or if the question, raised by the couple, arises at some previous appropriate time—I explain my position:

"I do not see myself as a savior of marriages, but rather as a person who tries to understand people and to help them understand themselves, each other, and their situation, so that they   95 can make better decisions about the course of their lives. While we come from the same culture, and I believe, as both of you do, in the integrity of marriage, I do not believe that human beings need to live the rest of their lives suffering the consequences of a mistake. Since at this moment you appear to have decided on divorce, my job now is to help you disengage in a manner least painful for everyone concerned, especially for the children.

When the decision to divorce is a genuine one, the spouse who makes the decision takes appropriate and effective action that permits the other at least to begin to adapt to clearly changed circumstances. Both can now take advantages of what support, knowledge, and experience the therapist can bring to assist them with the process of divorce.

Depending upon the character of their previous relationship I may say:

Divorce is akin to death; in some ways it's even more difficult. You are experiencing a loss, and yet the person you are losing is within reach. There is always a possibility that it won't happen or that it will be avoided at the last minute. Even if it does not at the moment feel like the loss of a person, at the very least it is a loss of previously shared feelings, aspirations, hopes, and goals. A sense of profound failure and guilt may well plague you for a time. It's not to be gone through without some kind and degree of hurt.

My treatment of those who are divorcing, however, does not differ in any major respect from my treatment of those who are not. Only the content of the material discussed changes; the goals change. If the couple do not themselves raise the question of how to handle the situation with the children, I introduce it, indicating my conviction that for their children the divorce represents a grave crisis. I emphasize that it is not the divorce as divorce, but rather how it is accomplished, how it is handled with regard to the children, and how it is explained that matter. Unfortunately, a few divorcing couples continue to be so self-centered, so hostile, so uncaring, irresponsible, or vindictive, that it is impossible to extricate the children from the imbroglio. These offspring are made into scapegoats by their parents or are used as pawns in their quite uncivilized chess game. To this state of affairs, our antiquated, fault-ridden divorce laws make a significant contribution.

For most patients who are divorcing, it is possible to attain a number of goals:

1. Assist them in reaching mutually acceptable agreements with regard to the division of property and alimony, as well as child custody, child support, and visiting rights.

2. Help them formulate a way of together explaining the situation to the children, so that it will be as a-traumatic as possible, for example, "We can't get along as husband and wife, but Dad will continue to care for you, and so will Mom; you won't lose either of us."

3. Support both of them assiduously to avoid belittling, criticizing, or blaming the other before the children. It should be "We made a mistake," not "Your dad. . . ."

4. Aid them in accepting the soundness of the attitude, although an older child may express a preference for living with either (as part of the legal process), that any responsibility for such a decision rests with the judge and that neither parent will regard such expression of preference on the part of the child as reflecting disloyalty. In this situation, the therapist may find that he has to offer ego-supportive explanations to the parent whom the child is partially rejecting, as to why that particular child may have made that decision.

5. Where it seems indicated on the basis of parental reports of a child's symptomatic or behavioral reactions, get the parents to accept the urgency of arranging promptly for therapy for the child.

97

If, at the end of therapy, I judge either or both to be still vulnerable to yet another inappropriate or impulsive choice of mate—whatever the unresolved reasons may be—I state my opinions and predictions of what is likely to happen and strongly recommend individual or group psychotherapy before anyone becomes seriously involved in another relationship.

When all or most of these goals have been achieved, I feel good about what we worked out together and consider the results good.

A Word of Advice

In my experience with myself and with those professionals who have consulted me about their clinical problems, I have found all too often that using a "new technique" consciously and deliberately may turn out to be a dud. When my eyes, or those of these others, have been focused on trying something new and interesting, I could not concentrate on understanding the needs of the patient. It is better if the therapist forgets all that he or she has read here. Instead, let whatever has seemed valuable in this book and whatever has been incorporated bubble up from within, stimulated by what the therapist and the patients are together experiencing.

BIBLIOGRAPHY

Books

Ackerman, N. W. (1958), *The Psychodynamics of Family Life*. New York: Basic Books.

Alexander, F., and French, T. M. (1946), *Psychoanalytic Therapy*. New York: Ronald Press.

Anthony, E. J., and Benedek, T. (eds.) (1970), *Parenthood*. Boston: Little, Brown.

Bergler, E. (1969), *Selected Papers of Edmund Bergler*. New York: Grune & Stratton.

Berne, E. (1966), *Principles of Group Treatment*. New York: Oxford University Press.

Brenner, C. (1966), *An Elementary Textbook of Psychoanalysis*. New York: International Universities Press.

Colby, K. M. (1951), *A Primer for Psychotherapists*. New York: Ronald Press.

Dicks, H. V. (1967), *Marital Tension*. New York: Basic Books.

Erikson, E. H. (1963), *Childhood and Society*. 2nd ed. New York: Norton.

Ferber, A., Mendelsohn, M., and Napier, A. (1972), *The Book of Family Therapy*. New York: Science House.

Freud, S. (1938), *Basic Writings of Sigmund Freud*. New York: Modern Library.

Greene, B. L. (1965), *The Psychotherapies of Marital Disharmony*. New York: Free Press.

Lewin, K. (1948), *Resolving Social Conflicts*. New York: Harper.

Lidz, T. (1963), *The Family and Human Adaptation*. New York: International Universities Press.

Parsons, T., and Bales, R. F. (1955), *Family, Socialization and Interaction Process*. Glencoe, Ill.: Free Press.

Tarachow, S. (1963), *An Introduction to Psychotherapy*. New York: International Universities Press.

Waelder, W. (1960), *Basic Theory of Psychoanalysis*. New York: International Universities Press.

Watzlawick, P., et al. (1967), *Pragmatics of Human Communications*. New York: Norton.

Wolberg, L. R. (1965), *Short-Term Psychotherapy*. New York: Grune & Stratton.

Zuker, H. (1967), *Problems of Psychotherapy*. New York: Free Press.

Articles

Ackerman, N. W. (1962), Family psychotherapy and psychoanalysis: The implication of difference. *Fam. Process*, 1:30–43.

Alger, I., and Hogan, P. (1967), The use of videotape recordings in conjoint marital therapy. *Am. J. Psychiatr.* 123:1425–1429.

Cohen, M. B. (1966), Personal identity and sexual identity. *Psychiatry* 29:1–14.

Fitzgerald, R. V. (1969), Conjoint marital psychotherapy: An outcome and follow-up study. *Fam. Process*, 8:260–271.

Fry, W. S., Jr. (1962), The marital context of an anxiety syndrome, *Fam. Process*, 1:245–256.

Giovacchini, P. L. (1967), Characterological aspects of marital interaction. *Psychoanal. Forum*, 2:8–29.

Gross, M. D. (1969), Marital stress and psychosomatic disorders. *Med. Aspects Hum. Sex.*, 3:22–33.

Grunebaum, H., and Christ, J. (1968), Interpretation and the task of the therapist with couples and families. *Int. J. Group Psychother.*, 18:495–503.

Haley, J. (1963), Marriage therapy. *Arch. Gen. Psychiatr.*, 8:213–234.

Jackson, D. D. (1965), Family rules. *Arch. Gen. Psychiatr.* 12:589–594.

McDermott, J. S., Jr. (1970), Divorce and psychiatric sequelae in children. *Arch. Gen. Psychiatr.*, 23:421–427.

Rashkis, H. A. (1968), Depression as a manifestation of the family as an open system. *Arch. Gen. Psychiatr.*, 19:57–63.

Rogawski, A. S. (mod.) (1966), Psychoanalysts view conjoint therapy. *Psychoanal. Forum*, 1:147–166.

Sager, C. J. (1967), Transference in conjoint treatment of married couples. *Arch. Gen. Psychiatr.*, 16:185–193.

——, et al. (1968), The married in treatment. *Arch. Gen. Psychiatr.*, 19:205–217.

Schmidt, S., and Liebowitz, B. (1969), Adolescents and their families: A treatment model combining family and group treatment. Reprints obtainable from the Family Institute of Chicago, Oak Park, Ill.

Strean, H. S. (1967), A family therapist looks at "Little Hans." *Fam. Process* 6:227–234.

Watson, A. S. (1963), The conjoint psychotherapy of marriage partners. *Am. J. Orthopsychiatr.*, 33:912–922.

—— (1969), The children of Armageddon: Problems of custody following divorce. *Syracuse Law Rev.* 21:55–86.

Wender, P. H. (1967), Communication unclarity: Some comments on rhetoric of confusion. *Psychiatry*, 30:332–349.

—— (1968), Vicious and virtuous circles: The role of deviation amplifying feedback in the origin and perpetuation of behavior. *Psychiatry*, 31:309–324.

Wenner, N. K., *et al.* (1969), Emotional problems in pregnancy. *Psychiatry*, 32:389–409.

Whitaker, C. A., and Miller, M. H. (1969), A re-evaluation of "psychiatric help" when divorce impends. *Am. J. Psychiatr.*, 126:57–64.

Zuk, G. H. (1968), Prompting change in family therapy. *Arch. Gen. Psychiatr.*, 19:727–736.

Suggested Readings for Patients

A therapist should, of course, be familiar with the contents of these so that his recommendations can be tailored to the needs of the couple.

Berenstain, S., and Berenstain, J. (1970), *How To Teach Your Child about Sex*. New York: McCall.

Goldstein, M., and Haeberle, E. J. (1971), *The Sex Book*. New York, Herder and Herder.

Harris, T. A. (1969), *I'm O.K., You're O.K.*. New York: Harper and Row.

Kirkendall, L., and Whitehurst, R. N. (1971), *The New Sexual Revolution*. New York: Donald W. Brown.

Kronhausen, P., and Kronhausen, E., (1968), *Erotic Art*. New York: Grove Press.

Lawrence, D. H. (1957), *Lady Chatterley's Lover.* New York: Grove
    Press.
Marshall, D. S., and Suggs, R. C. (1971), *Human Sexual Behavior.*
    New York: Basic Books.
Robbins, Jhan, and Robbins, June (1970), *An Analysis of Human
    Sexual Inadequacy.* New York: New American Library.
Rubin, I., and Kirkendall, L. (1971), *Sex in the Childhood Years.* New
    York: Association Press.
Siecus (1970), *Sexuality and Man.* New York: Scribner's.

APPENDIX A:
Illustrative Case History

M RS. R. A. made the initial telephone contact and told of longstanding marital problems and of a recent episode of marijuana smoking by their adolescent son that had "at long last" motivated her husband to seek help with their marriage. She suggested that it would be better for her husband to see me first since he would likely feel that she could prejudice me against him were she to come in first. I accepted her suggestion without comment, except to state that I preferred to deal with her husband directly and would call him after he returned from work that evening to discuss the matter of an appointment with him. When I did so he responded positively, and I informed him that I would put him in line and call again when a regular opening occurred on my schedule. After seeing the husband first, I alternated the couple's subsequent appointments.

Mr. R. A.'s history follows. Either I quote directly or paraphrase more concisely what the patient said; inferences made by me later or as I go along (usually by taking notes during the interviews) are in italics.

Presenting Problems

"I say things when not sober; drinking is my main problem and is getting worse. Also, I have trouble with my wife. We've had no sex for several years; she refuses because I drink and smoke too much and am too fat. (*Manner and voice tone is petulant.*) Two months ago when my wife called for an appointment our son had been picked up and charged with possession of marijuana; he was placed on probation and the court referee recommended that we get help with our marriage. I guess our problems probably started at least ten years ago."

When asked to clarify his opinion about his contribution to the marital trouble patient admitted that he was, "not 100 percent honest" with his wife and that he lied to prevent her from blowing up. He also labeled himself a spendthrift, wasting money drinking, and, "if I want a tool or something I want it right now and go out and buy it." When asked to be more specific about his alcohol consumption, Mr. R. A. replied that he drank three to four pints of whiskey per day. He denied that his drinking interfered with his job, which was of such a nature that he could regulate his own time and could go to work when he felt up to it. (*Probably his hangovers do interfere with his efficiency.*) The patient spontaneously tells about counseling with his minister ten years ago that helped him stay dry for two years. (*This would place onset of increased drinking and marital problems earlier than the ten years he previously stated.*)

Probable Precipitating Events

1. *For onset of difficulties, the pair's fertility problem, for which no organic cause was diagnosed, and husband's ambivalence about having children, which probably involved the adoptions as well, although he asserted he agreed with the plan to adopt.*
2. For seeking help at this time, their son's involvement with marijuana and the juvenile court.

Present Life Circumstances

The patient is forty-eight. He lives with his wife and two adopted children (daughter, aged sixteen, son, aged fifteen) in a modern seven-room home that they are buying. His job is at an executive level, and he is satisfied with the type of work he does and his income. He believes that his rate of advancement has been above average. About once a month he travels on company business and is away for four or five days. On these trips he regularly has sexual relations with a number of women; he says he knows one or two willing partners in each town he visits. He enjoys intermittently working around the house as a hobby and reads light escape novels. The couple belong to a country club, and he occasionally plays tennis and swims during the summer months. Mr. R. A. claims that his wife has refused to go out socially with him for several years because of her embarrassment about his behavior when he is drinking. He does not remember what he says or does. She reports it to him later.

Marital History

Mr. and Mrs. R. A. have been married for twenty-three years after a courtship of six years. Husband speaks in glowing terms of their courtship and early marriage. He says he was attracted to and remained interested in his wife because she seemed to be a very lovely person with a nice personality. He enjoyed being with her, and she, likewise, seemed to enjoy being with him. (*Mr. R. A. was unable to describe specific personality characteristics that led to his interest in his wife, except for the clichés described above.*) Pressing and probing were unsuccessful in eliciting more definitive information concerning mate choice. When I confronted him with his vagueness about this matter he became a bit irritable and stated that he couldn't remember details that far back. Asked his opinion of what his wife saw in him, Mr. R. A. replied that he had no idea and went on to describe his wife's disappointment, early in their marriage, when he did not finish college as he had planned to do. On the other hand he said that things went well for the first two years and that he could recall no trouble during the two years they lived in their first apartment.

Without being asked, he related that, after they decided on having children, he stopped having sexual relations with his wife. "Maybe I feared having children." After they resumed having relations, conception did not occur, and four years later they adopted their first child (both were adopted as infants).

Family History

FATHER The patients father is living and in reasonably good health for his seventy-five years. He is Protestant Lutheran. Mr. R. A. was unable to identify his father's background in terms of nationality. He was always "nice" to the patient, although he was irritable with mother during the Depression. He recalls many serious arguments and that they were very poor. The patient was not able to remember or even guess how his father felt toward him. "When we were older my sister told me I was my father's pride and joy. I was the youngest by eleven years, probably an accident, and the only son. My father and I had good times together; he was free with his tools and let me use them whenever I wanted. He played catch with me. He was a friendly, outgoing person. He encouraged my friends to spend time at our house. I had a happy childhood. Oh, I did resent my grandmother's (father's mother) interference, even when she took my side."

The patient apparently felt resentful about his being relegated to a less desirable bedroom because the grandmother had the best one in the house. Concerning the relationship and feelings between his parents as husband and wife the patient was either unable to recall or unwilling to reveal any concrete details about what passed between them on a feeling level, except for the arguments described above. He said only, "It was a beautiful relationship." Again *(defensively)*, he asseverated that he could not remember much about his childhood. When directly asked about his parents' use of alcohol, he replied that they drank only occasionally and never to excess.

MOTHER Died of arteriosclerosis ten years ago at age seventy. Her background (religion and nationality) he believed to be similar to that of his father. "She was nice, too nice, probably not strict enough." He supported this feeling with one memory of having stolen some money from her and getting only a *mild* lecture. He described her as very loving and indicated she showed her feelings through kisses and talking with him, "a normal relationship."

SIBLINGS The patient has two sisters, twelve and eleven years older than he. "They were very nice; we got along well as a family. My older sister liked to boss me; I liked the younger one better." As far as he knows, neither sister has or has had any emotional or marital problems, although contact with them is currently minimal.

Earliest Memories

AGE FIVE   Playing in a sandbox with his long socks filled with sand; a short time later coming down with pneumonia.

AGE ?   Death of his father's mother; her casket was in their home. His father gave him a rose to put into his dead grandmother's hand.

AGE FIVE OR SIX   He recalls that he got into "big trouble" when he threw rocks into a baby carriage belonging to a neighbor. "I probably didn't know the baby was in it."

Dreams

Recently—none. Repetitive—as a young child, preschool and after starting school, the patient remembers frequent nightmares of wild dogs or wolves tearing his mother to pieces, which he relates to his being enuretic then. These dreams were frightening enough to awaken him. Both dreams and enuresis disappeared when he was age seven or eight. Other nightmares—none recalled.

School and Occupational History

The patient completed two years of college in business administration. He was never a disciplinary problem in school, was a follower, and did not participate in sports or other extracurricular activities. Before his twenty years of employment with his present company, he held two other jobs, changing jobs to obtain better pay and opportunity for advancement.

Sexual Development

The patient could not even guess what his parents' attitudes about sexual matters might have been or what their love life may have been like. "It was never discussed; they gave me a book to read." He presumed that he learned about masturbation at age eleven to twelve and did so regularly with no conflicts, worry, guilt, or shame about masturbation (except for anticipated parental disapproval if he were caught).

While overseas in the Army during World War II (*an undistinguished career that he endured*) he suffered a slight wound and spent several weeks in a convalescent center. On leave from there he had his first complete sexual relationship with a prostitute; he experienced no difficulties except for minimal fear of venereal disease. After the war he lived with an Italian girl for several months and experienced a gratifying sexual relationship with her. In passing he mentioned that he first enjoyed getting drunk while in the convalescent center. He replied in the negative to questions about any homosexual experiences and said that he had never been approached. He said he would just tell the homosexual to "get lost," if he were propositioned.

Goals

"To find out how to get over my drinking problem and to have a more complete marriage." He had no idea how a psychotherapist went about doing therapy.

Observations

During the two interviews the patient appeared restless, often spoke rapidly to the point of stammering slightly, and chain-smoked. He was indeed moderatly obese and presented a somewhat sloppy appearance; his clothing seemed a size or two small. The patient was often vague and evasive when he attempted to answer questions raised by me. He expressed no affection for his wife, giving economic convenience and his concern about the effect of divorce on the children as his reasons for remaining in an ostensibly unrewarding marriage.

Impressions

This patient impressed me as a cold, hard individual, and I sensed him to be hostile and capable of cruelty. Part of this defensive facade may have been because he was subjecting himself to evaluation partially under duress. He seemed self-centered, impulsive, and defiant, and heavily defended against dependency. Access to childhood memories was limited *(repression?, deliberate witholding?)*. His earliest memory suggests some connection between pleasure *(autoerotic?)* and punishment, *(illness)*. His third early memory suggests hostility toward infants. The repetitive childhood nightmare, linked in his associations to enuresis, points in the direction of maternally directed hostility. Although he painted a diametrically opposite picture, I suspect that for him dependency equals control. Alternately, he may well have been pampered and had too few limits set, so that he became self-indulgent with few inner controls. His casual mentioning of his bossy older sister supports the former inference.

The dynamic picture here is, at the outset, unclear. His occupational history is a stable one, and, when sober, he apparently operates effectively and efficiently. Although I cannot be too sanguine about the prognosis, his favorable response to a little support from his minister ten years ago indicates that the outlook may be better than it seems at first glance.

Mrs. R. A. was seen for her first interview a week after her husband's first evaluation session. She gave the following history then and during her second individual interview.

Presenting Problem

Mrs. R. A. replied to my invitation to tell me of the troubles that brought her by summarizing her marital history in a rather well-organized way. She said that she must have been immature to have seen her husband so differently when they were going together from the way he later turned out to be. During their courtship she had judged him to be conscientious, responsible, and ambitious. She was also attracted by his "gaiety and charm." "I've always been a trusting person, perhaps too trusting." She had expected her husband to finish college after they were married; she planned to continue working until he obtained his degree. She felt betrayed when she learned that her husband had been expelled from school for nonattendance. "He skipped classes behind my back. He's dishonest with me many times and I've been a sucker." (*Weeps and apologizes for doing so.*) Mrs. R. A. cited several more examples of her husband's dishonesty and profligacy with money. "He's been alcoholic for fifteen years and is also obese. All of this seems like a lack of consideration and respect for me, even like he's getting back at me for 111 something." The patient linked her husband's increased drinking, which has escalated through the years, to about the time they adopted their first child. "Now after he has just one drink he has a personality change and accuses me of the most terrible things, like having homosexual relations with a girl at my office." (*The patient seems like a long-suffering martyr.*)

When asked about any awareness of her contribution to the troubles between them, the patient replied, "Basically it's a personality conflict. I believe in firm, consistent discipline. I think I pushed too hard for my values. I assumed too much responsibility, picking up after him, managing the budget so we could save something. I see now I should have soft-peddled in some places. Maybe we're just not suited for each other." Asked if there were other difficulties, the patient told of the behavior problems with their son, which she ascribed to the disagreements between herself and her husband that permitted the son to play one against the other (*seems introspective and psychologically minded*).

Probable Precipitating Events

1. For onset of difficulties, she ties the dramatic increase in husband's drinking with accompanying intensification of already existing marital problems to their adoption of their first child.

2. For seeking help at this time, Mrs. R. A. confirms husband's story with respect to this question.

Present Life Circumstances

The patient, age forty-seven, works as a private secretary

to an executive in a large corporation mainly to supplement their income. She expressed resentment that she has to work because of her husband's extravagances. Mrs. R. A. indicated that she would prefer to be a housewife so that she could devote more of her time to sewing and to her artistic interests. She also enjoys sunning, swimming, and walking in the woods. Confirming her husband's story, she expressed her negative feelings about socializing with him because of his behavior while under the influence of alcohol.

Family History

FATHER   Died in 1960 at age sixty-five of cerebral thrombosis. His nationality and background was Scotch-Irish and he was Protestant. He was a self-employed, successful small businessman. In early childhood she remembers him as affectionate but reserved about showing his feelings and somewhat stiff and formal. "Most of my memories about him are healthy ones. He was reliable. I was the third of four daughters, and we were able to do most of what we wanted to do. He was generous with us. He was responsible and conscientious and expected us to do our best and toe the mark. He was respected as a person in the community." When asked for more information about her father's feelings toward her, she reiterated that while she knew that he loved her and her mother, sisters, and brother, he did not show his feelings overtly. She described further her father as a very controlled person who only rarely showed anger. She volunteered that she married her husband against the wishes of both of her parents. They regarded him and his family as beneath them.

MOTHER   Living at age seventy-six, moved to Florida last year. She was a housewife who never worked out of the home. "Mother didn't like responsibility for the larger decisions. She left them to my father. She was fair and loving but not gushy. She expected things to be done and supported my father in what he expected of us. I was fond of her until, in my late teens, I discovered I didn't like her indecisiveness; it seemed weak. She left too much to my father. On the whole both of my parents gave me enough so I felt secure, and they gave me good character development."

SIBLINGS   The patient has sisters six years older, three years older, and five years younger. "We got along well, of course, the usual spats. I was the least prone to combat. I had a very good relationship with my younger sister; I was closer to her and took more care of her than did my sister."

Earliest Memories

AGE FIVE OR SIX   The patient recalls that she scared her younger sister by peeking around a corner and yelling "Boo" and that her mother scolded her for doing so.

AGE EIGHT   "I told my girlfriend about the birth of my younger sister; I was proud. She deflated me by saying that she already had one."

Dreams

The patient stated that she rarely remembers her dreams, and she could not recount any recent ones. She recalled one repetitive dream from childhood that was frightening. When attempting to run from some unknown danger, her feet felt like they were stuck in molasses so that she could not escape.

School and Occupational History

The patient is a college graduate. Although trained in a different field, she has been working as a secretary because the pay is better; It was necessary for her to go to work about eight years ago for economic reasons, as previously discussed. Mrs. R. A. excelled academically throughout her school career and was active in a multitude of extracurricular activities.

Sexual Development

"It was typical of our era. Our questions were answered graciously but incompletely. It wasn't talked about. We were told that we would learn about such things when we were older. Mother gave me a book to read; she would have been embarrassed to talk about sex or menstruation." The patient's first complete sexual experience was with her husband after marriage. Early in marriage, when she felt loving toward her husband, she says that she had a gratifying sex life, reaching orgasm, "most of the time." While her husbands's sex drive was stronger than hers in terms of frequency, she didn't, in those early days, mind giving him pleasure even when she was not in the mood.

Goals

The patient felt that she would be content if they could re–establish some sort of a relationship. "I believe that I should see it through, rather than upset the children more than they already are. We have had no meaningful relationship for years, and, therefore, I'm not at all interested in sex with him."

Further Information Volunteered by the Patient

"Dick has often complained about his grandmother who lived with them during his childhood; he complained about her being domineering. I also believe that he didn't respect his father, who was unemployed for a time during the Depression. Instead of trying to find a job, he just stayed home and did the housework.

"I don't like what I've become. I used to sing to myself and have a good time at parties, and I used to be witty. Now I feel dull and depressed.

"Since he read a sex book several years ago, my husband has considered me inhibited. I don't think I was, and I'm not now. It's just that the only time he approaches me is when he's drunk, and that disgusts me."

Observations

The patient was neatly and attractively, although conservatively, dressed. She told her story in an unusually well-organized manner. It was difficult (and sometimes impossible) for me to control the interview so that I could cover my agenda. When I attempted to change the subject to explore a different area, the patient ignored my move and continued until she was ready to move into that area. In contrast to her husband, Mrs. R. A. was able to be quite specific about both the recent and more distant past, giving examples to clarify points. She seemed slightly sad and weepy.

Impressions

Mrs. R. A. seemed strong-willed although not harsh. I

had the feeling that it would be easy to get into a battle of wills with her. Some awareness of her domineering tendencies was present. Dream material was limited to one that suggested both anxiety and a self-defeating trend. Both parents were strict, demanding, and controlling, especially the father. The marriage model the patient experienced with her parents was one in which the husband was in the dominant role. While this was apparently acceptable to the patient's mother and worked well for the parents, the patient didn't like it. I suspect this influenced her mate choice; she picked a man whom she felt (on some level) that she could manage. Her earliest memory suggests hostility toward her sister as well as maternal strictness. The second memory suggests that *she* may have felt deflated by the birth of her younger sister. As the patient's defensive need to be in the driver's seat with her husband progressively failed, she has become more and more depressed. Her son's delinquency has also contributed to her feelings of failure and discouragement. The fragility of the marital coalition must be intimately related to the son's behavior which has involved more serious things than possession of marijuana, e.g., vengefully destroying one of his mother's favorite lamps. On the surface it would seem that Mrs. R. A. is an intelligent, responsible, and conscientious woman valiantly attempting to cope with a couple of monsters. I wonder if she is not somehow acting as an *agent provocateur* in bringing out the "worst" in her husband and son.

Tentative Formulations about Their Relationship

I strongly suspect that one of the core transactional dynamics or vicious circles in the marital dyad will emerge along the following lines: Efforts on the part of the wife to get her husband to conform to her (conscious) expectations hit him on a sensitive spot. He reacts with rebelliousness and defiance (excessive drinking, spending sprees). This, in turn, arouses anxiety in the wife, who responds with increased efforts to control his behavior, intensifying his characteristic reaction, and so forth. Obviously, I could start the circle with the husband's behavior. The wife seems to be in a parental role vis-à-vis her husband's adolescent role and vice-versa. I wonder also to what degree the husband needs and is gratified by a controlling kind of "affection" and the wife needs and is gratified by the "acting out" that represents an alien, repressed part of herself.

This couple have probably been in a state of distress with this pattern for about fifteen years. The prognosis can only be regarded as fair. That the son's involvement with the court was, or seems to have been, the event that motivated them for therapy is puzzling. Their fifteen years of suffering without taking any action leads me to believe they share a need to suffer or feel undeserving of anything better. Their motivation for change does not seem likely to hold up.

Appendix B:
An Exchange of Letters

Dear Mary,

I feel somewhat foolish as I sit to write a letter and try to put into words feelings that for some reason I'm not able to express more directly. I can't understand at this point why I have so much difficulty with it, and my hope is that this can be a step toward helping us communicate more directly with each other.

Time after time Dr. Fitzgerald has had to point up to me how I don't share my feelings and how you can't be expected to do something different when you don't know how I feel. I agree that is a problem, but I also feel that you know some of the things that concern me and still it doesn't seem to get much better.

As I try to make sense of my feelings, I keep coming back to 119 the main theme, which is a feeling that you don't need me, and questioning if you really love me.

These are not mere idle words, but somehow I've not been able to communicate to you the depth of my feelings and the desperate situation our marriage and my personal life is in. Dr. F. compares it to being on the "edge of a cliff," and we go on trying to pretend that things aren't that bad. (I used this terminology in an individual session with the husband when the wife was absent for a legitimate reason.)

What I've wanted all these years of our marriage is for us to have more of each other but we've accumulated more things, while, in many ways, we have less of each other than we had before we were married. I feel I've tried very hard to please you, to perhaps make you want me, and to try to make you happy, but feel I've failed miserably.

As I sit here now and have done so often, I can't think of a way I feel you really need me or that I add anything to your life that couldn't be supplied in other ways or by someone else.

My income is fairly good, but you could get money from working, insurance, support payments, or probably other ways. The same goes for the other material things we have.

The only reason I ever feel you need me is to take the kids off your hands for an evening or for a couple of hours to give you a break. That could be done by a babysitter.

It is my deep feeling that the only thing two people can give to each other is themselves. If they don't have that, they don't have anything. The rest can be supplied in other ways. I DON'T KNOW HOW TO GET CLOSER TO YOU.

If I take seriously all the education I have had or the experience I have gained working with people, I have to conclude that I'm doing something that keeps you away, builds distance between us, and blocks your desire to respond to me in the way you used to do that I desire. I've tried to figure out the puzzle by myself and haven't been able to do so. You'll have to help. Your actions give

120

indication of dissatisfaction with me, although you say it isn't so.

When I want to kiss you, you turn your cheek or turn my head away. When I want to hold you, I feel you pushing me away or turning away yourself. When I want to fondle you and touch you I find you disliking it and not wanting me to do it. When I've begged for you to touch me or have taken your hand to place it on me, you have withdrawn it and communicated disinterest.

Our sexual relations are rarely satisfying to both of us. I get the impression that you consent to having relations because it's a wife's "duty" to do so from time to time but not because you either enjoy or need them. I don't know how to interpret or understand your lack of responsiveness and feel I'm not doing something to please you. I've wondered at times if you're saving yourself for someone else, since I don't feel you giving yourself to me. Sometimes I've asked what I can do to make it more enjoyable for you, and I don't get an answer. Maybe I didn't ask loud enough for you to hear, but I think I did. Your silence is seen as another rejection, and the hurt has built up inside of me, since I didn't know how to deal with it. Now I find myself turning away and not taking the initiative with you so I can avoid possible further rejection and hurt.

Although you look so pretty when you smile, much of the time you are scowling. I see you going around looking upset, being angry with me or the kids when it isn't clear what the anger relates to, and being frustrated and harsh for reasons that are not at all obvious. Any of us might ask what seems to be a reasonable question, and the way you respond make us feel our question was way out of line and "silly" or "stupid" and we shouldn't bother you.

As we've talked before, when you shrug your shoulders, I get upset and try to read in what the answer is. The same feeling occurs when you say "maybe" or "I don't care" or "What do you think?" when it turns out that you already had a good idea 121 *of what you wanted to do, but I didn't know. Even Jane (the oldest child) has said a number of times, "When Mommy says, 'maybe,' that usually means, 'yes.' " I guess it could be helpful, if you said, "yes" or "no," when that's what you mean.*

In an effort to try to make or keep you happy, I've been very sensitive to what does bring you pleasure and what does put you into a better mood. Head and shoulders above any other situation that brings you pleasure is being with your folks. Since that makes you happy I've gone along with a lot more visits and trips there than I've felt have been reasonable. I'm glad to see you happy, but then I'm hurt that I can't bring you any degree of happiness that approaches what you feel with them. I feel in competition with them for you, and there's no way I can get a silver or even bronze medal out of the competition. I, too, can enjoy them and appreciate all they've done for us, but when visits there interfere with developing friends here or when it comes through so strong that your closest relationships are with them and not with me, I get resentful, feel hurt, and at times conclude that the best way to help you be happy would be to leave you and let you move back with them.

I've thought a lot about the alternatives to working at a better relationship, but none of them look like solutions. I seriously considered suicide so you could be free to find happiness wherever that would be for you. I've been tempted to seek affection and closeness with other women but wouldn't be able to deal with the guilt that would cause. I've considered moving out or getting a divorce, but everything I know about that kind of an attempt to solve problems suggests it should be a last resort, to be pursued only after all efforts at building closeness have failed.

I sincerely do want our life together to be more satisfying for both of us, and I deeply desire a closer relationship between us in which we can both feel how we are needed by each other–so that if everything else is lost, we would still have each other and the uniqueness of the relationship we can develop.

122

I come begging for your help, 'cause I'm at the edge of a cliff and feel the sands shifting underneath.

Love,

John

Dear John,

Well, herè goes—this has to be the most emotional piece of literature I've written, whether it shows that way or not. I think I'll begin by answering your letter paragraph by paragraph.

Dr. F. sure is right—you haven't communicated to me past a point in your ideas or feelings. You say I know some of what bothers you and a little some it is. I know you want more open affection and a better bed partner. Beyond that the rest of the letter brought me SHOCK, sadness, and complete confusion along with a flow of tears; but you know about some of those.

You say over and over again in several ways how hard you've tried to please me and how unhappy I seem. Yes, you do try hard, perhaps, no, not perhaps, but definitely, too hard and leave your own self and personality to bow to me. You are always a source of strength when I need you (a place I've apparently failed you completely) and yet not strong enough to tell me "no" to something for fear it will hurt me or I guess that's it. Maybe it would, maybe I'd be angry, but I'd know what you want.

I need some help on this NEED business you speak of. What do you need that I'm not giving (besides the previously mentioned)? I need you just to be here and I can't imagine life without your coming home and just being here. Maybe, I don't know, this is a part of why I didn't realize the seriousness of your depression. My emotional needs appear to be so different from yours in my eyes.

You mention independence, getting along without you, etc. I would hope I could manage if I had to, but that is the farthest 123 *thing from what I want. Wouldn't you want me to be able to care for myself and our children, if necessary? I would hope that you could do without me, not with pleasure and not without a great sense of loss, but that you* could *do it.*

All my thoughts are mixing together and I fear rambling so much you can't understand. Besides it's hard to see through tears, so bear with me.

Something I fear you misunderstand in me is when I want you to do something for your own good and you see it as a "putdown" by me, e.g., when I keep saying "go and play golf–call someone" or "take that course in history you've been talking about" or "ride the bike, get some exercise." If I read you in these situations, you think I'm trying to get rid of you and I'm not–I feel everybody needs some time to himself *to do his* thing, *not his kid's thing or wife's or friend's, but* his *(or hers).*

The last time we were at Dr. F.'s together we got into the reasons it's difficult for me to express my feelings physically, and I'd rather leave it there until we go back.

That word suicide has been flashing around me like a neon sign for three days now, and it's still a shocker and so, so unsuspected. What did you ever say or do that I should have picked up on to realize how bad you felt? How can you even believe that would make me happy? Boy, our communications have been at the worst!

I'm sorry our jaunts to my folks have made me seem so different. I don't want that. As far as being grateful–I hear your brother here–he can't accept things done for him by his in-laws either but I thought you realized there is no commitment here to repay except as our feelings dictate. I expect if I were in the Boston area (husband's home) *I would feel like doing things for your parents just because they are your parents. I don't feel we spend that much time there* (on the farm) *any more, except for birthdays and holidays. This we must talk through with our calendar as* 124 *well as with our feelings.*

I do need you to be you—not as a clinging vine—that's not me and never was. I do need you to be here, so dear God, please realize this if nothing else here makes any sense—I love you, and I'm proud of the many times people say how wonderful you are. I hope I find the way to tell you often enough to make you know it.

I've felt for some time our religious life is backsliding, and all this makes my feeling stronger about that. Please, with my prayers, accept me and let me help you and myself to something more.

Love and tears,
Mary

Appendix C:

Interview 1

*T*HIS VERBATIM interview is included because it so dramatically demonstrates an extremely serious communicational problem. It is an initial conjoint interview and begins after I have made my usual introductory remarks. During the interview and while listening to the tape, the degree of confusion produced by the interrupting and simultaneous talking seemed much more profound than it does in the typescript. This is expectable, since the act of setting a dialogue down on paper requires a certain amount of structuring and organizing. As I have noted in my comments as I was dictating the interview from the original tape, I was sometimes unable to disentangle the dialogue and had to abandon my efforts to do so.

Throughout the interview I consistently attempt to treat the communicational problems. My efforts begin with an explanation and end with my powerful enforcement of turn-taking, like the chairman of a committee meeting. Thus, this session exemplified one of the subjects discussed in Chapter II under "Common Problems."

Husband: "We've been married eleven years now, and there are some things we don't have any problems on. We don't have any real major financial problems. Mary takes care of all the bills. I bring in the income, deposit it in the bank, and she manages it all from that point on. Initially, during the first year, we did have a problem. I was doing the check–writing and so on; she said I was overly cautious, and so I said "Okay, it's all yours." Do you have any comments there, as far as financial problems?"

Wife: "Only that I think you're a little tight. I've been very cautious about what I spend and even don't buy some things that I need. But since we've been coming to the doctor, you've said I could spend a little more. But I have been overly cautious, even frugal."

(Couples often make some changes during the three or four weeks it takes to complete the initial evaluation interviews, whether I have made any speculative comments about their dynamics or not. Usually I read this as responsive to the prospect of being looked over and judged by a person in authority. Overly dependent, approval-seeking people are quite likely to do so.)

Husband: "You have, there's no doubt about it. Since I put the management in her hands, she's done well, better than I have. So, I might be a little tight and a little cautious, but I don't think that's a major stumbling block.

128

Wife: "No, no, I wouldn't say it's anything major, I've

just got into the habit of spending less. Now I'm going to spend a little more."

Husband: "You have access to the checkbook, and you can use your judgment. So far as I'm concerned, if it gives peace of mind, you can spend a little more."

Wife: "I've just bought my first coat in eleven years, and that did make me feel better (laughing)."

Husband: "So, so far as financial things, I don't think we have a problem. You talk about marriage, you usually think about financial problems, sexual problems, and religious problems. So far as religious problems, I don't think we have any there, we're both of Protestant background, ahh . . ."

Wife: (interrupting) "Though it took many years for you to *finally* join the church after the children were quite old."

Husband: "That's true, but I don't make a point of thinking you have to belong to this church or that church. My own religion says that it's up to you, and if it makes you happy, you should be doing it. Otherwise you can do it yourself. You really shouldn't affect anyone else by what you believe, and I don't think I do. I was Methodist in background, but we now go to an Episcopalian church. And it's very convenient. It's more a matter of convenience, it's just across the street."

Wife: (interrupting and speaking simultaneously) "It's just a short walk."

Husband: "So far as the kids are concerned . . ."

Wife: (interrupting and speaking simultaneously) "It was your father who told you the kids should be going to Sunday School, wasn't it?"

Husband: "Maybe he did, but I don't think we made religion a real stumbling block . . ."

Wife: (interrupting) "Just think, it took me a long time fighting to get you to go to church. You said you were going 129 for me, and I wanted you to go for you, because you believe in God and because you wanted it for yourself. You go begrudgingly."

Husband: (interrupting) "I'm afraid if I went for me, I'd never make it, because I don't feel quite the same way. But, as far as I'm concerned, we both go together on Sunday mornings . . ."

Wife: (interrupting) "But, honey, I think marriage is a compromise, and if you want to be a loner on all of these issues, you can't be a loner and be married. If you're that much of a loner and a noncompromiser, you shouldn't be married. Because marriage is a compromise, and a wife has, she has fifty percent say-so—as much as a man. I don't think a man should dominate marriage."

(The wife's domineering trends couched in terms of sweet reasonableness are quite evident. It would be a mistake to attempt to move in on the interpersonal or transactional aspects of their relationship before the serious communicational confusion is modified. During most of the interview, both are quite tense, restless, and anxious.)

Husband: "Well, I think this is one of the lesser problems. I'm going to her church now, I started doing that last year. I think this was a significant step forward on my part, and I don't make any bones about it. I think I act peaceable when I go . . ."

Wife: (speaking simultaneously) "No, it's not a problem now, not now. It was, but not now."

Wife: (after husband pauses momentarily) "You don't speak to people like I do."

Husband: (simultaneously and interrupting) "That's my nature though. I hate to say it, but it really is."

Wife: "It comes across as unfriendly when you don't speak to them."

Husband: "Well, maybe I'm doing something that I shouldn't, but I'm going."

Wife: "That's right. Maybe you don't really like to go to church."

Husband: "Okay, but is that a problem?"

Wife: "No, but it's like all these things that you do begrudgingly, unhappily, and it takes the fun out of it for me."

Husband: "But don't you appreciate that I can have my own thoughts, my own feelings, and they don't have to coincide with your thoughts?"

Wife: "Yeah, but when you're begrudging feelings cause conflict in the marriage and cause me to get ill, and I have to go to the doctor and take tranquilizers to live with you, I don't think this is a very wholesome kind of a marriage—when one person is so dominant that they do just what they want to do, and it causes tremendous conflict with the other partner, who can't live with this kind of thing."

Husband: "You say that religion is a part of the whole big picture?"

Wife: "Yes, it's a little part of it. It's like everything else. We go out to a movie, you go begrudgingly. If we go out to dinner for my birthday, you go begrudgingly. And it takes all the fun out of it for me, honey. I'd just as soon stay home. I understand you're a stay-at-home kind of person and you're tired from your work, but a birthday is something different; a movie once a month shouldn't be too much."

(The husband seems to be in the child role vis-à-vis the wife's parent role. But again it would be premature to address this circumstance this early in therapy and in the presence of so much confusion.)

Husband: "So religion is a part of it, but I have my own thoughts. And I don't think you should put your wishes in front of anybody else."

Wife: (interrupting) "I did it, John, mostly for the family, for the kids."

Husband: (talking simultaneously) "For the example and . . ."

Wife: (continuing) "Eric (their oldest child) wouldn't go to Sunday School because you weren't going to church."

Husband: (interrupting) "So, we straightened that one out. I'm glad you told me."

Wife: "Yes, you don't go happily, but you go."

Husband: "So, there is a little problem there, but I don't think it's a major one. So, let's go on to the sexual area. I don't think there's a major problem there. I'm not speaking for Mary, but I don't think so. We have what I call a normal relationship. We agree. I don't think anyone inflicts anything on anyone else."

Wife: (interrupting) "Well, honey, it comes to this: You do what you want to do in your marriage, and so you're a happy person. You read the paper from five to twelve because that makes you happy, but that kind of upsets me."

Husband: (speaking simultaneously) "From five to twelve?"

Wife: "Yes, as soon as you get home from work. But, honey, I think we would be better off if we would both pursue a hobby in the evening. Maybe if you'd get at your woodworking, with all the nice tools you have, with those beautiful tools, and me with my sewing . . ."

Husband: (speaking simultaneously) "Sure it would, okay."

Wife: "But when I see you from the kitchen where I'm working, reading that paper all evening long—and you're so talented. You've got artistic talents . . ."

Husband: (interrupting) "I guess I'd better document my time with the newspaper."

Wife: "It's not just the newspaper, it's reading. It's *U.S. NEWS* or whatever book you might have. It's reading, what-

132

ever you have in front of you, the childrens' books (laughs). You enjoy reading, and I appreciate that, but it's that we don't have anything to show for our time."

Husband: (interrupting) "Well, if this is a point of concern, documenting it might help, keeping a diary, showing what kind of things I do around the house. I know it's not zero, but I know it's not a hundred percent either. There are things that she wants done, and I know they should be done, and they take a while for me to get to . . ."

Wife: (interrupting) "It's come to a point, after nine years of wanting a mirror put up in the bathroom, that I just go ahead and hire the carpenter and the painters and the plumbers. But it would be different if you weren't good at doing that kind of thing, if you weren't mechanically inclined, but you are."

Husband: "Well, I did some things around the house when I had a week's vacation this year. When you start something, you like to have adequate time and not start something that you can't finish or have to leave . . ."

Therapist: "Okay, I think I've listened long enough now to spot a problem in the way that you talk with each other. And as I am seeing the problem, it's like this: Before you have resolved the first item you brought up—no, I may be wrong about that, not the first item, the financial thing may be resolved, I'm not sure—but then you brought up a second item about religion. But then you left it. You left it before it sounded to me like you'd really resolved it, found a solution, resolved the feelings about it, and then you went on to another item, and another item. Now you're talking about mirrors in bathrooms and other things around the house, so you jump, jump, jump."

(I decide to intervene gently with an explanation and a reflection of how they are sounding to me.)

Wife: (at several points during the above explanation) "Uh huh, uh huh" (and at the end when I pause), "we had this kind of thing with my mother last week. I see what you mean."

Husband: (speaking simultaneously with wife) "You're right. We go on systematically before we isolate the problem. If religion is causing us trouble, I can change, I'm flexible. If I'm not outgoing enough, I can force myself to be. But it will be hard, I'm not an outgoing guy anywhere. True. It's not just at church. I'm not able to say 'good morning, how are you' and . . ."

Wife: (interrupting) "No, no, on vacation you can be the life of the party, you know how to get along with people; you can be beautiful."

Husband: "Okay, so I don't feel real comfortable in church, I can't be real natural there. I'm nervous and I'm uncomfortable, and I can't make small talk there. Sometimes it's better not to talk about things like politics and religion; it can get you in trouble."

Wife: (Throughout the above passage, wife has been interrupting and talking simultaneously with the husband, disagreeing with him. In response to this he keeps talking, getting louder as he goes. Finally she gets the floor.) "Let's see, you mentioned two things you can't talk about, politics and religion?"

Husband: "Well, I . . ."

Therapist: (interrupting) "Hey, hold it a minute. I think I see another problem. (There's a little laughter in my voice and they both laugh in response to this.) You know, you're going *so* fast. It's sounding and looking to me like you really aren't listening to each other. You're zip, zip, zip, zip, you're overtalking each other, like you're so locked into your own thoughts and so eager to get your own points across that you're not really listening to the other one."

(I can't recall what my mild amusement was all about; perhaps the absurdity in the situation got to me. In any event this intervention represents a bit firmer effort to modify their communicational pattern.)

Husband: "Yeah, I don't know whether you can detect it or not, but I'm very defensive. I feel like I always have to defend my position. When you're in that kind of a role, you're defensive."

Therapist: "Yeah, you're like a couple of lawyers in court. Instead of listening to what the other guy is saying completely, you're making up your own arguments."

Wife and Husband: (both laugh)

(I decide to reinforce the husband's germinal insight; I also hope to lower the anxiety level with a little humor.)

Husband: "We've been through this many times, and it gets pretty . . ."

Wife: (interrupting) "But should we get to the heart of the matter though?"

Husband: "Well, I'd like to eliminate those things that don't perhaps matter—the things that aren't jeopardizing the marriage . . ."

Wife: (speaking simultaneously) "Yes, but, but, but . . ."

Therapist: (interrupting) "Try to slow down now, try to slow down a bit and listen to each other. Let's try taking turns."

(This is a firmer suggestion to try to get them to listen to each other by taking turns.)

Husband: "We're trying to get our money's worth."

Wife: (laughing) "We're under a time limit. I think it's   135 going to take a lot more than one time. We are under time pressure."

Husband: "All right, if you want a resolution about going to church, I'll put an effort into being more friendly. I really will. But I don't really want to go to the point where I'm getting involved in religious things. At least at that particular church I don't feel I have that much to offer. And, number two, that kind of thing doesn't fit me. I don't think a little standoffishness really hurts, so long as I go set the example for the kids. And I don't really think it does anyone any harm."

Wife: "Well, Eric is just like you. He senses it. He doesn't like Sunday School. And he doesn't like church. But I don't really think that's the big problem. I think we're wasting our time with it."

Husband: "But, all of the little things add up."

Wife: "The big thing is your parents. You're not defending me and letting me know that you love me enough to defend me."

Husband: (interrupting) "Let's not jump the issue now. I want to see to all those little things that add up to one big hatred—not all the time but some of the time."

Wife: (interrupting) "Don't you think a conflict between personalities . . ."

Husband: (continuing) "No doubt about it, there's conflict in most marriages. But getting back to religion, if that's bothering you, I can certainly change."

Wife: "Okay, I can live with your standoffishness. They'll take you for what you are and me for what I am. It kind of bothers me, makes me a little nervous. The people look at you a little warily, you're tall, and it makes me nervous."

Husband: (simultaneously) "Yes, I am tense. Dr. Fitzgerald noticed that right away. I am high strung, but once I relax-
136 —and it takes me a little time to relax—I can get into it.

I'm walking like on a high wire all day, and it takes me a while to relax . . ."

Therapist: (interrupting) "Just a minute. Let me check something out on your side of it, John, to see if I can learn something. Did you hear what Mary said about your going to church together?"

(In this comment and the three that follow I am trying to more concretely confront the husband with what he has not heard. Wife did make a small concession, although it was mixed in with a lot of other stuff.)

Husband: "She said that the big thing was about the example I was setting for the children, that was. the important thing. I think that's what I detected, that I should be setting an example, and I agree that's an important thing if it gets to the point where it's affecting the children. And I agree that we should be both going."

Therapist: "Did you hear anything else?"

Husband: "Other than that I'm standoffish in church . . ."

Wife: (interrupting) "I was hoping you would go because you wanted to go, rather than because I wanted you to go. I thought that you were going for the wrong reasons. I thought that you might go because you needed it."

Therapist: "No, hold it. That's not what I meant. I thought I heard you say to John, Mary, that . . . "okay, it was his personality, if he was a little standoffish and you were more outgoing, that the others at church would accept you as you were and accept him as he is." So you kind of made a concession, that it upset you a little bit, but you could live with it. And because you were talking at the same time she was, John, I didn't think you heard her say that."

Husband: "Oh, I heard her, but I don't believe that's what she meant."

Therapist: "Well, you didn't seem able to feed it back to me."

Husband: "I heard what she said. It is a small part of this big thing, and I think we should get it resolved. If you really feel that way, it's okay."

Wife: "I've told you that before, honey, but you know me. I'm so verbal . . ."

Husband: (interrupting) "If you really mean that, and if you're willing to forgive and forget, well . . ."

Wife: (interrupting) "I do love you and want you to grow."

Husband: "Yeah, okay, if you really mean that. But if you're imposing something on me, I think that's pretty basic, and we're never going to make it."

Wife: (interrupting) "It doesn't really bother me."

Husband: "If it's just learning how to tolerate my thoughts, and I . . . tolerating yours . . ."

Wife: (interrupting) "I'm tolerating it, and people smile at me. And they're looking at you warily, but I'm tolerating it, and I'm getting used to it."

Husband: "But you're saying I should change. And if you mean change my beliefs, that's pretty basic, and I'm not going to do that. That would be imposing on me. I've got my own beliefs and thoughts, and I'm going to keep them."

Wife: (speaking simultaneously) "You can change if you want to."

Husband: (continuing and speaking simultaneously) "I don't put them on you, and I don't want you to put them on me."

Wife: "I have to say I'm pretty open. Maybe I'm too naive, and people hurt my feelings."

Husband: (speaking simultaneously) "You're an extrovert, ah, ah, yes, that's part of the problem. Okay, but I'll make a point here. Again, don't impose on me. I'll go, I'll go with a smile, and I'll go for the kids . . ."

138   *Wife:* (interrupting) "You're involved with Rev. Smith.

You know what a nice person he is."

Husband: "Yes, in his own house, he's real down-to-earth. But when he's up there in the pulpit, he sounds like another person altogether. But you think I should be changing in my beliefs, and if we can establish that . . ."

Wife: (interrupting) "No, it's not that I think you should change so much, it's that I can't live with you the way you are (laughs). I guess I could live with you as long as I keep taking medicine."

Husband: "That's what we're here to do, we're trying to resolve that. But you're not willing then to accept me the way I am. You can't accept me the way I am."

Wife: "No, honey, I can't in everything. It's not just that . . ."

Husband: (speaking simultaneously) "We were talking about the religion thing . . ."

Wife: (speaking simultaneously) "It's not just that, it's . . ."

Husband: (also speaking simultaneously) "We're talking about religion right now. If you can say about that, yes, you can accept me . . ."

Wife: Okay, I can accept that you're going for me. But in my heart I wish you were going because you wanted to go for you."

Husband: (speaking simultaneously) "I can go, I can believe some things. I can believe there is Somebody up there. But I can't believe everything . . ."

Wife: (interrupting) "I can't believe everything either, John . . ."

(Because they are talking simultaneously and interrupting, it is extremely difficult to transcribe everything.)

Wife: "Well, I think we better get back to your mother and father."

Husband: "Let's just get to the things we might be able to get resolved first."

Wife: "Then you mean you plan to come again for another session?"

(This came as a surprise to me. Then I remembered that I had neglected to cover the question of a contractual commitment to a reasonable length of therapy earlier on. Usually I discuss this at some point in the individual sessions by raising the question of their expectations about therapy and correcting any misapprehensions about duration, if necessary.)

Husband: "I don't think we're going to make it all in one. I don't think there should be any intention of trying to rush it."

Wife: "Okay, okay, I thought you were only going to come once."

Husband: (interrupting and speaking simultaneously) "We've been having trouble for eleven years . . ."

Wife: (simultaneously) "Okay, okay, with some of them continuing, it will take many more times."

Therapist: (interrupting) "Hey, let's slow down and talk about that some. With people who have been married for as long as you have, who have been in conflict for as long as you have, I would suggest that you would need to commit yourself to therapy for a reasonable period of time for therapy to be able to be in any way helpful to you."

Husband: (speaking simultaneously) "Oh, I agree."

Therapist: (continuing) "And by a reasonable length of time, I would mean a minimum of six months."

Husband: "Well, I say okay, if it takes that long. We've been at it for eleven years, not continuously, but off and on. It must be something like phases of the moon, the way we go up and down."

Wife: (interrupting) "No, John, it's probably the disillusionment I had when we first got married, that . . ."

Husband: (interrupting and speaking simultaneously) "Well, that is more than we can handle today, believe me."

Wife: (Continuing, and it is difficult to hear everything she's saying.) "And if it hadn't been, we might not be together."

Husband: "Let's just look at the positive things, the things we might get resolved."

Wife: "Well, if you want to look at the positive things, then do you want to get to the other things later?"

Husband: (interrupting and speaking simultaneously) "Well, naturally, naturally, however it comes . . ."

Wife: "Evading the issues, well, okay . . ."

Therapist: (interrupting) "Let me share my thinking with you. As you've been talking about something you say is not a major problem, I'm sensing that Mary is having a problem with this churchgoing thing of the following kind: It's almost as if it isn't enough if John puts the best possible face on he can and goes. It's that he has to like it too. It's like it has to be something that is almost perfect."

(Having confronted the husband with a problem he has in listening, I now balance things out by attempting to confront the wife with her need to have things exactly her way, although I put it more tactfully than that. I attempt to deal with the wife's defensiveness with humor in my next statement and then with a direction, asserting my authority, in my third comment.)

Wife: (interrupting) "You're saying that it's wrong for me to think that way?"

Therapist: "No, I'm not saying that it's wrong. I'm saying that it is something important to take a look at. Say, have you guys ever gone to an opera or a ballet and seen the 141 wife of a couple sitting there, thoroughly enjoying it, and then taken a look at her husband and seen that he is sitting there with a transister radio earphone in one ear? He is listening to the hockey game, and he is only there to please his wife. Maybe next week, even though she hates it, she will go to the hockey game and be there with him, just to please him. She's there, and she's hating every minute of it, but she's returning the favor. And it's seeming to me that you're very sensitive, that John has to be there in exactly the same way you are."

Wife: "The reason it bothers me, Dr. Fitzgerald, is that it's not just this one thing, it's in everything in our life. He does everything begrudgingly, and I know why that is. He's exactly like his father, a stay-at-home, and it's natural for a man to be like his father, but . . ."

Therapist: (interrupting) "Hey, Mary, relax. Relax and leave the analyzing to me. That's my job. You've probably been doing that for years, and it doesn't sound like it's been much of a success. Why not relax and 'eave that to me?"

Wife: "Yes, okay, I took psychology, maybe that's why I do it. But Dr. Fitzgerald, I'm sensitive about John and religion, because it's the same in everything that we do together, isn't it, John? Everything you do in life, you do begrudgingly. And I'm at the point where I'd rather go to a movie with my mother than with my husband, and I want to go with my husband. I want to go with him because he's my husband. And I don't want to get in the kind of life where we're doing things alone. Maybe I'm looking too far ahead, but I said to John, "What are we going to do looking across the kitchen table at each other when the children are gone?" They're the only thing that has held us together, that we share, and he loves them dearly. He loves them more than I do. They are his whole life. And when they leave, there's going to be a very big vacancy."

142

Husband: (interrupting) "Well, you might be jumping a little ahead there when you said . . ."

Wife: (interrupting) "Well, but, honey, you said that you'd dump me when the last child was twenty-one . . ."

Husband: (interrupting and laughing a bit) "Well, we'll get to that . . ."

Wife: (interrupting) "Well, that's a fear hanging over my head. If you're going to dump me, you should dump me now, when maybe I can find another man."

(Again they interrupt each other and speak simultaneously. It becomes virtually impossible to transcribe the tape accurately.)

Husband: "Let's get back to the church thing. I'm willing to go, smile, and shake hands. I can and do enjoy people generally. I can be that kind of a guy. But sometimes I have a hard time communicating about things like religion."

Wife: (interrupting) "Do you think you have to talk about religion when you go to church. What do people talk about there? How are you, what have you been doing, how's your golf game?"

Husband: (interrupting) "I'm not that kind of guy that gets so interested in people, especially if they're strangers."

Wife: (talking simultaneously) "You don't have to talk about religion when you go to church . . ."

Husband: (interrupting) "I'm not that type of guy that can talk to strangers like that . . ."

Wife: "But you weren't remote to those ladies in the straw market. They were strangers, and you could talk with them."

Husband: (speaking simultaneously) "Let's get off the straw market . . ."

Wife: "But, I mean, I mean . . . but in one situation I think you have a built-in animosity about going to church, so you're going to be standoffish . . ."

143

Husband: "No, it's not animosity. I feel like I'm doing something that I can really do and get into if it's for the good of the family and will help keep us together. I'll go to church, I'll join the church, I'll take you, and I'll do all the things that . . ."

Wife: (interrupting) "And I'll accept you . . ."

Husband: (continuing) "Symbolically I can't . . ."

Wife: (interrupting) "Remember, we used to argue about it. And Rev. Smith told me that the children should be going to church, but you would tell them not to go. I would say, "No, John, it's not safe for them to stay home alone.""

Husband: (speaking simultaneously) "No, no, I never did . . . (then getting the floor) I've got my own thoughts about when a kid can get something out of going to church. Maybe you get them first by habit, and then it takes. But as I look back, I wonder how much good it did me . . ."

Wife: (interrupting and speaking simultaneously) "But Eric could beneifit just from seeing you do it."

Husband: "Well, okay, we can work that out, I'll really try. I'm already making an effort."

Wife: "You're making a very good effort."

Husband: "I'll do my best, but I can't be entirely comfortable there, even though I know some of the people, because historically I used to be with the Boy Scouts there . . ."

Wife: (interrupting) "Well, I can accept that. You're going, but you don't have to like it. You don't like it, and that's all right."

Husband: "You mean you really accept me?"

Wife: "Well, haven't I? Haven't I been saying it. And do I say anything to you after church? I don't think that's a hang-up now."

Husband: "But you're so anxious to get on to the thing that's really going to . . ."

144   *Wife:* (interrupting) "You're afraid to face it."

Husband: (simultaneously) "No, I'm not. I think we ought to take it in good time . . ."

Wife: (interrupting) "Yes, you are."

Therapist: "Again, see how difficult it is for you. You're so tense, you're like a couple of machine guns" (I make a noise imitating a machine gun.)

Husband: (speaking simultaneously) "Yeah, yeah, we've been at it so long . . ."

Wife: (speaking simultaneously, laughing) "Right, we've been at it so long . . ."

Husband: "Okay, so we'll try to slow down. And about the religious thing, we'll try harder and give you some feedback about that."

Wife: "I don't really think that's very much of a problem." (Again they are interrupting each other and speaking simultaneously, so that the overall effect is confusion.)

Therapist: "Hold it, ladies first. You, John, settle back with me and listen. Mary, I would like you to spell out what your position is with respect to going to church, fully and clearly while John and I listen."

(Other measures having failed, I now become very firm and directive.)

Wife: "Okay, I think he's going to church all right now. For years it was a conflict, and I was upset about it. But I think that's solved now. I'm satisfied now. I'm glad, and now I feel content about it."

Husband: "You feel . . ."

Therapist: "Shhhhhh" (hushing husband). Try to keep listening, John; Mary, go on until you are finished."

Wife: "Yeah, I thought for a while it bothered me when he didn't talk to people. But then I thought wait, they'll judge me for what I am, and they'll judge him for what 145 he is. So if he doesn't speak, he'll have to live with that. I can be myself and act friendly. They've invited us to the Couples Club, and I've been very honest and said that my husband is not interested. And I'm not apologizing about it, and I don't feel badly. I just say my husband is not interested in that kind of thing. He did lead the games at the church picnic, and he was just wonderful. He's a tremendous leader."

Husband: "Not really."

Wife: "Oh, yes, you are, you're a born leader."

Therapist: "Okay, are you finished now?"

Wife: "Yes."

Therapist: "Now, did you understand what she said?"

Husband: "I think so."

Therapist: "Okay, now let's change it around. Now, Mary, you and I are going to listen as he makes his statement of position as it is right now, today."

Husband: "Okay, I will. I'm going to try to appear to enjoy it. And I'm going to be as friendly as I can be, but that's as far as I'm willing to go. When it comes to a matter of beliefs, I can only believe what I believe. But I'll go and do my best, especially if it's good for the kids. Every week it becomes less difficult. Sometimes it feels like I belong there. I suppose that someday I'll even be taking the collection. I'm sure I'll go that far. But when it comes to getting involved in the politics, I don't want anything to do with it, because it doesn't really . . ."

Wife: "Ahh . . ."

Therapist: "Shhhhhh."

Husband: "I don't think they should be that organized, their getting so organized that it seems like a business."

Wife: (after a pause) "No, I agree. I don't want to get too involved either. It's okay to get involved with the Cub Scouts. We both are, but I don't want to get more involved than that either."

Therapist: "Okay, now it's sounding to me that once you can really settle back and listen to each other, then you can hear what you're saying, what your positions are, and that way, you can really get it resolved. At least with that problem."

(Now I move in with reassurance and praise to emphasize and reinforce the importance of listening rather than interrupting and talking simultaneously.)

Husband: "Yes, but I'd like a reading in a few months to make sure that she really means what she's saying."

Therapist: "Okay, we'll have to wait and see, so we can take a reading on that later.

(I wish to prevent an argument about what the wife will do in the future. What follows indicates that my move was unnecessary, since they seem able to discuss it without regressing to their earlier communicational process.)

Husband: "The one thing that I don't want you to do is tell me that I don't believe, don't believe in the right way. I do believe in God, and I'll have to wait and see if you're going to say those kind of things again. I don't think that anyone knows the ideal way of believing or doing anything."

Wife: "Neither do I."

Husband: "I don't think it makes any difference if you're Lutheran or Presbyterian, or Catholic, or what."

Wife: "Neither do I. And remember when we had that adult education course, I should have spoken up. Some of those people were picking apart the Catholics, and I said to you, John, I wish I would have spoken up and said, "Aren't we all Christians?"

Husband: "Yes, this is part of the reason I have objection to some of the churches nowadays."

147

Wife: "But like you say, honey, there is no perfect religion. There's no perfect church because there are no perfect people. No organization is going to be perfect if it's business, religion, or what, because they're all made up of imperfect people."

Husband: "Right, I agree with you there." "But we really will have to take a reading later, to make sure that you don't say things in front of the children about my belief like you have."

Wife: "We don't have to believe exactly alike. There are many things that I'm not sure of, like heaven and hell, and I don't think it makes that much difference. And I don't think we have to believe exactly alike."

Husband: "Well, I want the children to believe exactly what they see. When I look back, we went to church, that is, kids and mother, and sometimes I wonder how much good it did me. Our kids, I'd like them to go through the system and be able to make up their own minds about it—to learn on their own what's right and what's good for them. And I don't think they should be told to believe or be told by you what Daddy believes."

Wife: "Do you think you might have felt differently if your father had gone with you, as a family?"

Husband: "I think we've got it worked out now, just so you don't criticize me to the kids."

Wife: "I never did after you started going. I did before you were going and that was how many years before you joined the church?"

Therapist: "Hey, just a minute, there seems to be a little confusion. What I'm hearing is that John is asking you not to criticize his beliefs to the children in front of the children in the future. And you're going back to what you remember about the past. That's what he's worried about, your possible criticism of him in the future. And that's what he has to wait and see. So that he's telling you that it would bother him in the future if you do it."

(This comment, like the subsequent two, was designed to make a definitive separation between past and future as they talk in the present.)

Wife: "Well, when they'd ask me questions, I'd have to tell them the truth. I'm a very honest person. I wouldn't cover up."

Therapist: "Yeah, but what about the future?"

Wife: "Well, okay, in the future, if they ask me about you, or something that you're involved with, I'll tell them, "You go ask Daddy." That way, they'll get both sides of the story. They'll learn what you feel and what I feel, and then they can make up their own minds."

Husband: "That's exactly as it should be."

Wife: "Well this is one of our smallest problems. I didn't even think it was a problem until today."

Therapist: "Religion isn't really the problem, it's the way you guys deal with it. Like when you were talking about the future and you were talking about the past. Then you're not on the same wavelength."

Wife: "Yeah, we never are."

Husband: "You shouldn't say that, that's a generalization. We're not going to solve everything at once. We've got to take it one problem at a time."

Wife: "Well, that one is taken care of, you go to church and act the way that you act, be yourself, and it's all right with me. I don't care even if you take a transistor radio along with you during services (laughing)."

(Prognostically, this statement by the wife is favorable. She has been influenced in a constructive direction by my earlier humorous remark.)

Husband: "I'm glad to get that commitment."

Wife: "And if the kids ask me about what you believe, 149

if you believe in heaven or hell, then I'll tell them to go ask you."

Husband: "That's exactly the way it should be, that's exactly the way you should handle it."

Wife: "Okay, that's how I'll do it."

Therapist: "It sounds to me like we can go on now. It sounds like that issue may be resolved."

(I had apparently been so involved with being directive that I neglected to watch the clock or I would not have suggested that we could move on to another topic.)

Husband: "Well, let's go on then. Let's take up the next issue."

Therapist: (interrupting) "Our time is up, and there isn't time for another subject right now. You'll have to save that for the beginning of the next hour if you wish. We'll meet at this same hour next week."

Interview 2

This is the eighth session with the couple whose first interview precedes. Because I had been on vacation this interview occurred ten weeks after the first one, and my opening remark reflects the fact that we missed two sessions. I have included this interview to demonstrate the changes that can occur in such a short time. Note that there are only four instances of the couple's speaking simultaneously. When it does happen it does not seem to affect the flow of the communication and does not lead to confusion. During the intervening interviews the tension and hostility between the patients had been gradually decreasing. Perhaps this does not come through as clearly in the typescript as it does in the actual sessions or through listening to the tape. On the latter the voice tones and volumes can be heard. In the former the body postures, gestures, and facial expressions can be directly observed as well.

Therapist: "It's been a while. What do you have on your minds to talk over with each other today?"

Wife: "John was saying while we were on the way here that we pretty much covered everything, and I feel the same way too. But there are one or two more things I have on my mind. Are there any on yours?"

Husband: "My mind is a blank."

Wife: (laughing) "Your mind is a blank. I have a couple of little things. You're doing a beautiful job remodeling the bathroom, but I know that you are busy and have only so much time to work on it. I was wondering if you would mind if I would hire someone to do some of the papering and painting that needs to be done so that it wouldn't take up your time. What do you think about that?"

Husband: "We will have to discuss that. I can do all of those things; it is just that I am not as quick as you would like."

Wife: "Well, but would you mind, if we have the money to have a paperhanger or painter come in and help out? Our remodeling projects have been going on for years."

Husband: "Well, what's bothering you now?"

Wife: "Mike's room and our room. The paint is peeling again. You know we have that moisture problem there. I know there is a lot to be done, and you are busy and tired, And I was thinking if we have the money I would take over, get in touch with the men, be there when they come and see that it is done right. Would that bother you?"

Husband: "I don't see that there is that much to be done, that I can't do it. If you would help with the preparation, I could do it. The actual painting and papering I could do. It is not that difficult and I think that it would be great to work as a team."

Wife: "We tried that before with the outside of the house, and it still took a long time. I know that you are tired and . . ."

Husband: (interrupting) "With my job and my part-time business and all the work that needs to be done around the house, I don't like to be working all of the time. It seems at times that all I do is work."

Wife: "I undestand that."

Husband: "But if you would help, I still think that we could do it."

Wife: "No, you know what happened before. You love yard work, and you are very good at it. Gardening is sort of a hobby with you, so once the nice weather comes in the spring you won't have time to do anything until all of the yard work is done in the fall."

Husband: "I didn't know it bothered you that much that . . ."

Wife: (interrupting) "It does. It does."

Husband: (interrupting and laughing) "You should have married a combined plumber, carpenter, paperhanger, and painter."

Wife: "I understand that you are busy and tired. And I suppose that I ought to help more. I know that some women do paint, but it seems that I don't have the time either. By the time I take care of the kids, do the shopping, cooking, and all of the housework, I don't seem to have the time either. I am slow, too. But when we get done, it looks beautiful; but it takes about two years for us to finish anything" (laughing).

Husband: "I think we should plan things more, plan to do things together like agreeing to do so much on a Saturday. And then if that doesn't work out, we can hire some of the bigger things done like the house painting on the outside."

Wife: (interrupting) "I don't mind working together, but whenever I suggest that we do the painting, you say, no, you are not going to paint over this weekend as you have something else to do. Painting is one thing you hate to do."

Husband: "I think that we can discuss this out and reach an agreement about it. We don't have to spend the time here doing that. What's the next problem?"

Wife: "We haven't finished with this one yet."

Husband: "Well, I said that it is my responsibility, but I would like to request your help. Just with the preparation. Sanding is the world's worst thing for me. Painting itself is no problem. You did it before. You did all of the windows on the inside, and that was a great help."

Wife: "Yes, I did. I did that when the children were very young. But it wore me out and I sometimes wonder, if you have the money, if you should wear yourself out like that . . . if you have the money and you can hire some of it done."

Husband: "I don't get that tired. I can live with it."

Wife: (interrupting) "Well it wore me out, because I kept working right up until suppertime."

Husband: "I would like to try it again—getting you involved—and then if we find we can't handle it, we can talk about going outside and bringing somebody in. Okay?"

Wife: "You don't think that time has proven that we can't get it done?"

Husband: "I know it looks different to you, but it doesn't look that bad to me. But I know that you want things just right, but the way the house looks doesn't bother me."

Therapist: (interrupting) "Okay, the way it is sounding to me is that you are very close to reaching a compromise. As I understand it, Mary, if you would give it another good try in helping out with the work that needs to be done, and if it proves that you can't manage it together, then John would be receptive to hiring some of the work done. But I do have something to say about this, not about compromising, and I must say that you two do seem to have learned very quickly how to talk better with each other. You are taking turns, listening to each other, and talking with each other in a much more calm and reasonable way than you did a short time back. I like to illustrate the point I have to make about the house by telling you about a cartoon I saw in a magazine some years back. In this cartoon, which was of two couples, cavemen and cavewomen, the two women were standing inside the cave, which was very tastefully decorated with pictures, bric-a-brac, etc. while the two men were standing outside the opening of the cave and one was pointing out into the jungle. It was obvious that the two men were talking about hunting, fishing, or something of that sort. While inside the cave, the two women were talking with each other, and one said to the other, 'Did you have a decorator or did you do it yourself?' I think that cartoon beautifully demonstrates the difference in the feelings and attitudes that men and women have about their homes. This is a very, very difficult thing for men to understand. Women have been the nest builders from way back into the earliest times of our human history, while men have been more focused on what is going on outside of the house. This difference is difficult for women to understand, too. With a woman, it gets almost to the point of, 'If you neglect my house you are neglecting me; you won't care about *me*.' "

(In this comment I hope to accomplish three things: (a) cement and make final the budding compromise I have detected in their interchange so they can move on; (b) praise and thus reinforce their progress in terms of turn-taking and listening to one another; and (c) foster an understanding of each other's attitudes by generalizing about the common differences between male and female roles and attitudes.)

Husband: (interrupting) "She lives in it. She is in it much more than I am."

Therapist: "Right. Exactly."

Husband: "Yes, I can see that you are right about that. Sometimes I get the feeling I am not consulted enough, and I feel that as the wage earner you should at least listen to my ideas. There are many examples where you just went ahead without asking, and I don't think that it has to be quite that way because

(They do move on to another and more important issue.)

Wife: (interrupting) "Well, I feel, and maybe I am wrong in this, I do not know, but it is more my house. That the house is my work just like the X corporation is your work."

Husband: (interrupting) "But you have that home through . . ."

Wife: (interrupting and speaking simultaneously) "Through you. Yes, I agree, but one compromise I would like to see. I am willing to listen to you, but I would like to do the decorating. It is not that I am better than you, but I do read the decorating magazines and study."

Husband: (interrupting) "She is a very good decorator. Her brother is a decorator, and she works at it. You are a better decorator for others than for us."

Wife: "I think I am good for us too."

Husband: "You are, but I think you should consider my opinions. I live there, too."

Wife: "I still think that I should do the picking. I have to live with it more than you. I have to clean it, wash it. And I think you should pick out our cars. When we were buying that car in 1968—and maybe I was wrong to do this—I expressed my opinion that the Ford had a better pickup than the Chevrolet, and you were angry about that and you picked the Chevrolet."

Husband: (speaking simultaneously) "And we still have that car."

Wife: (continuing) "And you were angry that I didn't agree with you. But as it ended up, the Chevrolet wouldn't pull our trailer when we bought it."

Husband: (interrupting) "And I have heard about it for five years."

Wife: (continuing) "So this is the compromise that I would like to reach. I will promise to remain absolutely mum about the car decisions, if you will agree to let me make the house decisions and stay out of those."

Husband: "I think we could both be in on both of them. I don't like that compromise. We still have that car, and it works allright."

Wife: (interrupting) "But it won't pull the trailer."

Husband: "Yes, but we didn't have the trailer when we bought the car. And now every time the car chugs a little bit I hear from you about it. You can't forget it. It is enough to hear about something once."

Wife: "Do you think it is a compromise, Doctor?"

(It would be a mistake to respond in any way to the wife's invitation to side with her until I'm ready to do so. Note that the husband is apparently expecting me to side with his wife; he responds to her so quickly I'd have to interrupt to do so.)

Husband: "Well, I don't think it is a workable compromise. If it is my chair that is involved, I have to sit in it, and I think I should be able to have the say about which chair it should be. I don't mean color or anything like that, but the kind of chair that it is. And it is okay with me if you pick the color of the car, but the car itself, I should. But I wouldn't just pick a car without talking it over with you."

156   *Wife:* "I am going to still stick to what I said here."

Husband: "You are dealing with some pretty stubborn people here."

Wife: "I don't think I have ever picked a chair that wasn't comfortable. That red chair of yours is."

Husband: "Do I ever object? Do I ever make any noise?"

Wife: "Yes, when you first get it. But I know that it is going to last for just a few minutes so I leave the room."

Husband: "Do I for months and years continue the discussion of my objections?"

Wife: "No, you blow up, and it just lasts for a few minutes. That one time you pushed me."

Husband: "No, I didn't."

Wife: "Then maybe you forgot that you did."

Husband: "Well, I have had to live with that decision for five years now. I will be happy when that car wears out so you can sell it and forget it. But I suppose the next time, unless I agree with you and pick the car you want, I am going to be in deep trouble from then on."

Wife: (interrupting) "No, no, you pick whatever car you want and I won't say anything about it. Doctor, is that a compromise or not? Am I wrong in wanting to pick the furniture so long as I pick comfortable things for him? I keep his size and frame in mind when I buy."

Husband: (quickly) "I don't really care about most of the stuff—the carpet, dining room set, and stuff like that. But even with those things I like to be told. I want at least that much consideration."

Wife: "But I do tell you. Don't you remember, even with the furniture for the back porch, I talked with you about buying wrought-iron furniture."

Husband: "Okay, right. On that one we went out and looked at it together."

Wife: "This seems to be a standstill. Am I wrong, Doctor?"

Husband: (quickly interrupting) "You are very stubborn, and, then again, I have my own ideas."

157

Wife: "I think we need an objective opinion here. Is it wrong—if we agree upon the amount of money—if he picks the car and I pick the furniture?"

Therapist: "A compromise is only a compromise if both people agree to it. It is not for me to say how you should run your lives. It is not for me to say whether it is right or wrong for you to have the exclusive domain within the house and he to have exclusive domain over purchases of cars. That is none of my business. I think what is important is that you both be satisfied with whatever agreement you reach."

(The reason for spelling out my position is self-evident.)

Husband: "I think that if we buy a car, we should do it together. What's the point of doing it independently? That is the reason we are married, to do things together."

Wife: "Well, okay. But when I did give you my opinion about the car you were very mad. You told me I was stupid, that I was dumb. But as it turned out, my opinion wasn't so bad."

Husband: "I could give you example after example where you have made the final decision—like the bedroom suite—and I live with those decisions and don't say anything, do I?"

Wife: "As I said, you might blow up at first, but you forget about it."

Husband: "You describe me as explosive, and I don't think I am."

Wife: "You have ranted and raved, and you did push me."

Husband: "Well, how many times has that happened?"

Wife: "Two or three times. Remember the one time you pushed me, and I hit against the wall, and the children were crying."

Husband: "I can't remember that. I can't remember why I would do such a thing?"

Wife: "You said that I could buy it, so I went with my mother and bought it. And you said that you didn't like me going with my mother, so you took it out on me that way."

Husband: "It's our house and not hers. It would be better if you would go alone or invite me."

Wife: "There were times when I lied to you just to keep the peace."

Husband: "If you can live with it, go ahead. But the only objection I have is not being consulted."

Wife: "When you say I can pick something out and then complain about it later is when I consider it unjustifiable behavior on your part."

Husband: (interrupting and talking simultaneously) "These are all material things, and I see no reason to get excited about it." (Gaining the floor.) "You picked that rug and it has been shedding for years, and I haven't complained about that, have I?"

Therapist: "Hey, you guys. It seems to me that you are permitting yourselves to get all mired down in the past, so that you can't plan for the future and find ways to avoid similar troubles in the future."

Husband: "Yes, we are mired in the past."

Wife: "Yes, we do want to avoid that. Now, this has been a problem with us for years. So much of a problem that I have talked it over with many other women, and most of them say that they pick things for the house. So it seems to me that that is normal."

Therapist: "Well, I have an opinion to offer about that. I think that it depends on each personality involved, how they feel about it together as a couple, and how they work it out. So far as I am concerned, I don't care about the decorating. My wife and I have an agreement that neither of us *159* will spend more than a certain number of dollars without consulting the other. So long as I am consulted about how much it is going to cost and determine whether we can afford it or not, I don't care whether my wife has the wall painted black, blue, pink, or purple, or whether she buys this couch or that couch.

(Through the use of self-revelation I emphasize the importance of individuality, mine, my wife's, and each of theirs.)

Wife: "Uh ha, uh ha, I can see that."

Husband: "You mean, if you are painting it, you don't care whether it is black or brown or what."

Therapist: "Well, I have retired from painting. It is too much of a hassle. But then again, that's my personality. So that I think what's important for you to understand, Mary, about John's personality, is that he lived throughout all the impressionable years of his childhood in a household where the father had the last word about almost everything and where the mother–wife was extremely acquiescent. And that is what he is used to, that's what he needs. Now maybe he can modify that some and think that, maybe just because that's the way it was with mother and father, it doesn't have to be exactly that way with us. But he did live with that for a very very long time."

(During the husband's initial interviewing it was evident that he was strongly identified with his father whom he both admired and feared. This is the first opportunity I had to use this information interpretatively, since it took this long for the communicational confusion to clear. I hope to induce some empathy within Mary for John but also to suggest that John need not necessarily remain rigidly in the father-identification mold.)

160   Wife: "Yes, yes."

Husband: "And her's was exactly the opposite."

Therapist: "How do you mean?"

Husband: "Your father didn't have much to say about anything."

Wife: "Yes, but he wanted it that way. It wasn't that he was being dominated."

Husband: "But my position is . . ."

Therapist: (interrupting) "Hold it. You have just said a very significant thing about Mary. Mary, I think that you are basing your expectations about the way marriage relationship ought to be on what you saw and experienced with your mother and father in exactly the same way John is basing his on his experience with his parents and that these two sets of expectations clash."

(Here I emphasize and underline the other side of the coin and give the husband credit for having come upon this understanding on his own.)

Wife: "That's right, that's exactly right."

Husband: "We have been very stubborn. We have been doing that for ten years. But I refuse to get excited about most of these material things. I don't care whether a carpet is blue, brown, gold, or what, but it has been an irritation that it fuzzes so much. It gets all over my pants all of the time."

Wife: "Honey, yes, I understand. With you it is the rug and with me it is the same way with the car. They are irritations."

Husband: "It's so much of a bother I would just as soon buy a new one."

Wife: (interrupting) "It cost over $1,000.00, and I know it is a bother. But I think we should live with it as it's got some wear in it yet."

Husband: "It is getting less as it gets older, but every 161 time you vacuum it, it fuzzes. I wasn't consulted, and I have to live with that."

Wife: "But I did. I brought all of the samples home and showed them to you."

Husband: "Yes, but you picked it, and I wasn't really consulted."

Wife: "I don't want to sound like I know more than you do, but sometimes your tastes don't reflect mine at all."

Husband: "I am not at all fussy about things like that. She picks out all of my clothes. I could care less. You are always there with me, and I say, Mary, do you like this or that."

Wife: (interrupting and laughing) "Well, you won't even go shopping unless I push you. You were down to two pair of pants, and they were pretty shabby."

Husband: "If I didn't have my wife to keep me straight, I probably would be the world's biggest slob, so I appreciate that."

Wife: "No, you wouldn't. You're very neat really. You just don't care about clothes."

Husband: "No, I don't, and it is the same with things around the house. I don't care that much."

Wife: (laughing) "That's right. You're more interested in tools or an air compressor."

Husband: "Well, I think a good compromise is that we do things together. When it comes to the car, I want you there. I want you to like it, and I want you to like the color."

Wife: (laughing) "Well, I want to have something to say about the engine. I like the engine too. It bothers me everytime we are trying to pull the trailer and the engine goes chug, chug."

Husband: "Well, we are still having a problem with that. You see she never forgets."

Wife: "Well, that is the same with you and the carpet. You never forget about that—the fuzzing of the carpet."

Husband: "Let's look at some other examples, like my chair. You didn't consult me about that."

Wife: "That was a Christmas present."

Husband: "Okay, forget about that one. What about the dining room set?"

Wife: "We went together on that."

Husband: "It was a mutual decision?"

Wife: "You didn't say which one you liked."

Husband: "Well, I want to be consulted, and I want to be considered."

Wife: "I do. Remember the couch for the living room. You said that that pattern and fabric was the only one you liked and the only one you could live with, so I built the entire living room around that."

Husband: "I don't remember it just exactly that way. I don't think I was that definite."

Wife: "Yes, you were, John. Yes, you were, but I understand now—that so long as we consult together and get each other's opinion, it is okay with me if I have the pick of the house things and you get the car."

Husband: "Yes, and then we have to learn to live with it. You have to learn to live with it and not keep remembering it and bringing it up. Every time we take the car out, the engine chugs a little bit, and then I hear about it."

Wife: "I will make a promise. I will keep my mouth shut. I will never mention it again."

Husband: "And I will make the same promise about the carpet. Anyway, it doesn't really bother me that much."

Wife: "Well, it does bother me. It bothers me more than you complaining about it does. It is my mistake, and I can live with it."

Husband: "I don't mean to rub it in."

Wife: "You have mentioned it, but not as much as I have the car."

Therapist: "Well, I don't know how many times each of 163

you have mentioned the rug and the car throughout the years, but so far as this session is concerned I think they have each been mentioned about equally." (Husband and wife both laugh.)

(This represents an example of keeping the focus on the here-and-now of the interview, rather than depending on reports about what has gone on at home. It also says, in effect, "Your score appears to be even" and by implication, "Let's move on.")

Wife: "Right."

Husband: "Bad judgments we have both made we haven't been able to forget, perhaps."

Wife: (interrupting and speaking simultaneously) "Yes, we have to learn to be mature enough to forgive and forget. We live and learn. We live and learn, and we have to not rub it in! Learn to live with our mistakes. We are going to live with the carpeting and the car until we get better ones, next time, after they are worn out. We are only in our thirties, and by the time we are in the fifties maybe we will have learned more."

Husband: (laughing) "That's a deal. I'll be happy as long as I can have my yard and my shed. My shed is my shed, and I can do with it what I want."

Wife: (laughing) "You sure can. You built it, and you can decorate it completely. Can we now talk briefly about disciplining the kids? I get a little tired of it, and maybe you can help me out a little more. I am old-fashioned, and maybe I expect too much."

Husband: "That's why I stay out of it. I think they get enough from you, maybe too much. Not that you are not doing an excellent job—you are. She does 90 to 95 per cent of it, and I only do 5 to 10 per cent. But the reason I don't
164 want to get involved is that if I do then they would be getting

105 per cent and added to yours, that would be too much. Most of the time they do the right thing. Occasionally, they do the wrong thing. I am more tolerant of that than you are, and overall they are good kids and you do a good job."

Wife: (interrupting) "But maybe if I would let up a little bit you would . . ."

Husband: (interrupting) "I'd take over a little more. Yes, then I could."

Wife: "Right, okay, I would like that."

Husband: "But it is difficult for me to make judgments as to when to get involved and when not."

Wife: "A lot of times you don't even notice. When you are reading the newspaper, they could run right over you and you wouldn't even know it. They could be running all over the furniture and you wouldn't hear" (laughing), "and I could be in another room, in the kitchen washing the dishes. Maybe some people are more alert than others, and I hear it and I yell, 'John, John.' And if I yell out enough you say, 'Huh, huh.' It's wonderful to have a one-track mind like that; I wish I did. I'd probably be a better mother if I did, but I tend to be too observant. I hear them, and I am always afraid a lamp will be knocked over, or something will be broken, or that they will cut themselves. Our boy has been cut two or three times, and we had to take him to the emergency room."

Husband: "Sometimes I get blamed for that."

Wife: (speaking simultaneously) "Yes."

Husband: (continuing) "I was that kind of a boy. I used to fall down a lot, break a bone or get cut and have to go to the hospital so I guess I don't get excited about things like that."

Wife: "Well, I do think that a parent has a responsibility to guard the child from getting hurt."

Husband: "You are doing a fine job."

Wife: "Yes, but I would like a little help."

Husband: "If you back off, I will move in a little."

Wife: "Okay."

Therapist: "I think that on your own you have hit upon a very important thing. If I am understanding you, it runs like this: If you could do a little less, he would be able to do more; and if you could do a little more, she would be able to do a little less."

(Again I give them credit for discovering another of their vicious circles. I have pointed out two or three similar ones in previous sessions.)

Husband: "Well, as parents, we can't be as objective as we should. I think we have to depend on outside sources. I don't mean relatives, in-laws, or people like that. I mean teachers. And we get very good reports from the teachers about our kids. I think we have to depend upon that. If a kid is that good in school, he just can't be a bad kid."

Wife: (interrupting) "That's right."

Husband: (continuing) "That's the kind of thing I use for feedback, so that if you will back off . . ."

Wife: (interrupting) "Well, I have tried that. I have tried to wait, and I look at you and you haven't even heard what is going on."

Husband: "And I have to be more alert."

Wife: "That's right."

Husband: "I have to really work on it, but she is doing a fantastic job. She is really a good disciplinarian."

Wife: (laughing) "Yes, but I get pretty tired of it. But it is a common thing, and when I talk with other women they say the same thing—that their husbands are spending so much time and are so busy making a living that they are too tired to get involved with the children, with their discipline, so that the mothers are becoming the main disciplinarians. But I find that the children will listen to John much more than they will to me, because he is not with them as much as I am. They tune me out, and, of course, he is stronger."

Husband: "Yeah, and it is the same way with me. Something is not very likely to sink in when you come to it the third time around."

Wife: "Yes. Being with them all of the time, they don't pay as much attention. And a mother does get tired."

Husband: "Well, you don't look tired. You don't look that worn out."

Wife: "Well, maybe I don't show it."

Husband: "When it comes to kids, she is perfectionistic like other things, and there ain't no kid who is perfect. You do have pretty high standards for everybody."

Wife: "Yes, I do. But I have come down quite a bit over the past ten years, but those high standards probably are my biggest fault. I expect too much of other people and of myself so I must lower them. I am working on it."

Husband: "We do seem to be going through a peaceful period."

Wife: "I am feeling much better, and I would like to keep it this way."

Therapist: "I think I can confirm what you are saying. The atmosphere between you does seem considerably more friendly, less tense, less antagonistic. How do you account for this?"

(I wish to confirm their perceptions, which appear to me to be accurate, and to encourage a search for more insight. Usually this kind of question also stimulates a virtuous circle in which each gives the other credit for the changes.)

Wife: "A lot of problems that have been bothering me for a long, long time have been resolved."

Husband: "No, not completely resolved but getting discussed. Our communication has just got to be the biggest key. We have discussed things with friends and relatives before, and that's just no good. It doesn't work. I wish we could do it without you here."

Wife: (interrupting) "Well, I think we are learning."

Husband: "Well, I hope I can continue to have enough interest to discuss it with you. Usually, I used to just walk out."

Wife: "Right, right. That's what we have to remember so that there is a carry–over from here to home, so that we can sit on the couch at home."

Husband: "For the past two weeks, we have some candlelight in the dining room. It's an entirely different atmosphere. I like it much better than when we used to sit in that little cubicle I built in the kitchen. There is more room to spread out, and it is more comfortable and we can talk. It is kind of nice that you set the table and put out the candles."

Wife: (laughing) "Yes, yes, it is better" (laughing). "When I first did it, the kids said, 'Are we having company? Who is coming over?' And you took me out to dinner and a movie on Saturday night."

Husband: "Yes, but we have got to keep thinking of different things. We have got to look at new approaches."

Wife: "Wouldn't it be a goal for us to keep in mind to try to do like we do here and discuss something until we reach a conclusion and arrive at something that is satisfactory to both of us."

Husband: "Keep calm, try to keep our voices down, and keep in mind we are trying to reach a goal, a conclusion, like we do here."

Therapist: "I agree. It is very important to have carry–over from the sessions. Therapy isn't much use unless you can learn the tools to do the same thing at home that you do

168

here. That's why I think that every couple, whether they drink or not, should have a cocktail hour periodically through the week—husband–wife time—for serious talk just like your hour here. And if you don't take it, steal it, block it out, it just won't be there, the time to talk about things before they build up to explosive proportions."

(Part of this was intended to reinforce conclusions they had already reached. The latter part about blocking out time was intended to be directive and a warning. I have found that couples tend to procrastinate about arranging a "therapy hour" at home because so many other things, even the average expectable administrative functions of family living, interfere.)

Wife: "Right, right."

Husband: "We used to get into loud arguments. The only thing I could do would be to leave the house and stay out for awhile."

Wife: "Yes, and that was so frustrating when you would walk out in the middle of something."

Therapist: "It is frustrating, but at times it is better to do that. The atmosphere may be too hot to deal with an issue, so that it is better to leave it for awhile and then later come back to it."

(Here I wish to support the husband's walking out when the atmosphere gets too hot. He has lost control and acted out his anger physically on two or three occasions. But I also wish to support their returning to the issue when they both calm down.)

Wife: "Yes, but we never came back to it. We just left it."

Husband: "That's because you never cooled down; we couldn't come back to it."

Wife: "That's looking back to the past again, and we must 169 look forward to the future. Let's make that sort of a rule, what's done is done. Let's look forward to tomorrow. What can we change tomorrow to make things better?"

Husband: "You're doing that. You are learning how to fill your time. You signed up for the course in crocheting. That makes it easier for me, so that I don't have to entertain her as much as she used to want me to. She is doing her own thing, and I will entertain her once in a while. If I think of our house as being like my office, I can understand how you can get feeling caged in. There are times when I have to get up and walk around, just go anywhere, go to the head or something, something, just to get out of there for awhile."

Wife: "You really do that kind of a thing at the office?"

Husband: "Yes."

Wife: "I am not that much that way. My house doesn't bother me that much. If I had a choice between going out and doing something and staying home and reading, I would stay home and read. I am more of a loner, more of a quiet person."

Husband: "Well, I thought that when you complain about the paint peeling and things like that it meant . . ."

Wife: (interrupting) "No, it doesn't mean that. I don't feel caged in the house, like you do, so that things get to bothering me. It's only when something like that goes on for years that it bothers me."

Husband: "Okay, I was only suggesting that it might relieve you if you had more entertainment out of the house during the day. And then you wouldn't depend upon me so much for getting out."

Wife: "Well, that's the way your mother did it. She said that she couldn't stand being at home, that she couldn't even stand being with your father, so she got herself a job."

Husband: "Well, I don't intend to tell you how you ought to live your life. You don't have to do it like my mother did it. It is just that I was thinking that if things get to bothering you—the house, the kids, work—that if you could get away from it and forget about it and have some fun . . . do your own thing. But it is only my suggestion, and you can do with it what you want."

Wife: (laughing) "Right."

Therapist: "Well, I am sure it is well intended, but what might work for you might not work for her."

(Again I stress the importance of individuality, here of defensive protective measures.)

Wife: "That's right."

Husband: "Well, it affects me, it affects our way of life, if she doesn't find other outlets."

Wife: "Do I really bother you that much?"

Husband: "Sometimes. Sometimes it is hard for me to sit and read and relax. I get to thinking about repair jobs that need to be done, the paint that is peeling and those things."

Wife: "You look relaxed. Are you really thinking about those things when you are sitting in there reading?"

Husband: "I think of that list of yours. She has a list of things that need to be done, and it must have forty or fifty things on it."

Wife: "I keep that list for myself."

Husband: "I thought the list was for me. Paint this, fix that, paper that—you should see it."

Therapist: "Well, I can tell you one thing, John, painters and paperhangers are cheaper than psychiatrists."

(This does sound like gratuitous advice and siding with the wife. The only thing I can say in my own defense is that it didn't seem to do any harm. Occasional mistakes usually don't.)

Wife: (laughing) "I told him that myself."

Husband: (laughing) "You're sure right about that."

Therapist: "Well, time is up for today, so I'll see you next week."

Interview 3

The following verbatim interview is an initial conjoint session with a couple who have been in a chronically unstable marriage for nine years. They are high school graduates from working-class families. Married previously for about five years, the wife has two children from this first marriage; the discipline of these children has been a source of disagreement and conflict from the outset. On two previous occasions the wife had filed for divorce but did not follow through. The present referral was at the initiative of the counselor at the domestic relations court. At the initial evaluation session the wife agreed to have the divorce proceedings put aside for at least six months in order to give marriage therapy a reasonable trial.

Mrs. P. had been under psychiatric care twice before for "depression" and had been hospitalized on a private psychiatric unit and later in a state hospital. Total time spent in the hospital was about one year. Treatment was with electroconvulsive therapy and supportive psychotherapy. The main thing that she claimed to have learned from her therapist was not to hold her feelings in. I observed no depressive affect during my individual interviews with her. She seemed bitter, antagonistic, and angry.

Mr. P. had been seen by the wife's psychiatrist and the social worker at the state hospital only to talk about his wife's condition. Throughout their marriage Mr. P. has held two full-time jobs, one as a laborer and the other in a semiskilled capacity. He acknowledged that he was a jealous and possessive person but felt that he had been driven to this position by his wife's sexual involvement with other men. In her individual sessions the wife denied sexual or emotional involvement with these men, and I believed her. Both impressed me as more interested in fixing blame than in developing an understanding of their relationship. I felt that they would not continue for more than a few sessions. These predictions were confirmed by the course of events.

This couple arrived for their first conjoint session approximately fifteen minutes late. As they entered, I inquired if they had had any trouble getting here. The wife replied that they had purchased a new car and were held up at the Title Office.

Therapist: "Okay, since this is our first joint session, I think an introduction is in order. These sessions with both of you here will be quite different from the earlier ones when I met with each of you alone. During those sessions I had to gather as much information as I could as quickly as possible and as efficiently as possible, so I had to raise a lot of questions, kind of keep a tight control over the interview, and not turn you loose very much. Now it's time for me to shift my gears, settle back, watch, listen, and think, so that I can come to understand some things that are going on between you and within you that you may not be able to see. Actually none of us are, because you are too close to the situation and your feelings also get in the way. So, toward that end, I will encourage you to try to permit me to "fade into the woodwork" or to pretend that I am invisible or something and talk mainly with each other. And then whenever I have a question to raise, a comment to make, or an explanation to give, I will interrupt and do so. Now, there aren't many ground rules. We've already discussed fees; I think that I have told you that I require at least a twenty-four-hour notice of cancellation to avoid payment 173 of fees. From this point forward, this will be a joint therapy. I will not be meeting alone with either of you unless the three of us decide together ahead of time that there is some good reason to change the plan of meeting together regularly. (Wife interrupts at this point, taking a form from her purse, tells me that they have major medical insurance that covers this form of therapy, hands me the form. I confirm that this is the proper form, agree to fill it out, and explain the usual procedure in submitting bills to the insurance company.) Now, let me see, I was talking about ground rules—there is a pledge that I will make to you. I shall, at least as far as humanly possible, maintain my neutrality—that is, I will not be partisan, take sides. Now, that does not mean moment-to-moment neutrality, I may agree at any one particular moment more with one than the other. However, over the longer haul, I would make every effort to balance it out and not take sides. I would also ask you to feel free to tell me if it seems to you that I am siding with one of you more than the other, so that I can take a look at my feelings and what I am doing and correct any mistakes that I am making along this line. It is possible for me to "slip my gears." I have just one more thing I would say to you now that I am ready to turn the floor over to you two. And that is that I encourage you to speak mainly to each other, so that I can do what I said earlier—that is, listen, watch, and think. Okay, I'm ready to turn the floor over to you two now, and remember, anything goes, except breaking up the furniture!"

Wife: "What shall we talk about?"

Therapist: "You two may pick the topics."

Wife: (to husband) "What do you want to talk about?"

Husband: "I just got out of bed. I just woke up."

(He works the night shift and sleeps for three or four hours before therapy sessions.)

Wife: (looking at Therapist) "A lot of the trouble with John and me goes back many years; he doesn't understand me. He's pointed out many things that stuck in his mind. He doesn't trust me, which is the big thing."

Husband: "It's not that I don't trust you, it's the way you do things."

Wife: "The way I *have* done things."

Husband: "If you've done them before, you can do them again."

Wife: "If I will do them again. But you don't believe that I didn't ever do anything that wrong."

Husband: "When I'm gone as much as I am gone, it doesn't seem to me you have to be running around like that."

Wife: "But where am I usually?"

Husband: "I'm not saying you're always out. But when you're gone, I'm at work."

Wife: "The big night in question is the night I go bowling, and that's only one night I have out a week to bowl."

Husband: "After you go bowling, you always go somewhere else afterward, and that's where the trouble is. Like when that man called the house the day after you were bowling—things like that there. You always go somewhere else after bowling."

Wife: "Not always, but when you go back seven years and the situation in our house then—the way we did all that fighting. And I told you, if a person is happy, he's contented to stay at home. So then I wanted to be somewhere else. And it wasn't that I was with another man, I was with a woman who knew a man who had a friend."

Husband: "And you all four were together."

Wife: "No, the man, whom I might add—and I told you before—was old enough to be my father, and he mentioned that he worked at your plant. You know that I'm an outgoing person. I talk to everybody. I can't be rude; I'm not that way. He wasn't trying to pick me up, he just mentioned he worked at your plant. And I said, "My father and my husband work there too." The man called the next day, and I have no idea why. I told you that before, and that's been seven years ago."

Husband: "Well, you was out awful late; you must have been doing something."

Wife: "One night when I came home from the bowling alley with another lady—and you know Jane—a man she met there followed her home because, you know, she was a bit under the weather. And when they stopped at our house, I got out of the car right away. He asked me to give him his New Year's kiss, and—and I told you this—I told him that I was not that kind of a woman. And you've elaborated on that ever since. It's these little things that I want to tell you about that you're not understanding about. So, therefore, I have to bottle everything up inside and maybe tell my girlfriends or people who I think are understanding and won't be critical. I don't necessarily want them to side with me, but just so they won't be critical, just so they'll listen."

Husband: "In turn, you wouldn't want me doing it."

Wife: "No, I wouldn't want . . ."

Husband: "You know where I'd be staying if I done it. As a man, I feel most men have an ulterior motive in wanting to kiss, or hold hands, or something like that. I know there's good and bad in everybody. I know there's good and bad in everybody, men and women . . ."

Wife: "If you respected me as a person, you wouldn't want to believe the worst."

(I believe the wife has been vengefully flirtatious and provocative but not unfaithful.)

176   *Husband:* "Well, when a man calls the house, and when

I'm at work, and you have your ex-husband over to the house . . ."

Wife: "Right, he came to the house, and I didn't invite him. And I told you about it."

Husband: "But at that time in the morning, you shouldn't let him in."

Wife: "You know he was playing on my sympathy at that time because he knew—and I didn't tell him, it was common knowledge among our friends—that I had filed for divorce because you beat me up. You know that he had two children there and that deep down in his heart he felt that I might come back to him with his two children—that I would go back to him because I was so unhappy. I feel—and I told you this before way back—that I'm not the only one who has damaged your trust in people, that there have been others, both men and women; you don't have as much of a trust in people as I want to put in them. I may be very wrong and very stupid in trusting people. You know I'm gullible. I've learned over the years not to be quite so much, but I still . . . because I never really try to look for the worst in a person."

Husband: "So put yourself in my shoes. If it had been the other way around, what would you have done? You know what you would have done."

Wife: "But I told you, I would have never stayed out late if I wasn't already mad. And it doesn't make any difference that I was with Jane, just because of the kind of life she lives. I don't have to live the same kind of life; and I like her as a person. At one time while she was divorced she was a mistress to a man we both know. But this made no difference to me; it's none of my business, and this didn't make her a common, ordinary streetwalker. I don't blame her. There are circumstances behind everything, and maybe she needs psychiatric help."

Husband: "Still, if it would have been me, it would have been altogether different."

Wife: "I don't think you would do those kind of things."

Husband: "That's the difference between you and me; you don't find me running around in bars."

Wife: (talking simultaneously, overriding husband's last statement) "I'm not, I'm not."

Husband: (continuing) "You don't find me running around and going to bars."

Wife: "You have stopped and had drinks after work, John. You've stopped and played pool."

Husband: "Yes, but not like you do."

Wife: "You make it sound like it's all the time. It's not; it's once a week, maybe I do. Sometimes it was only for a cup of coffee, and usually all last winter I was home by ten-thirty."

Husband: "That's because I was babysitting for the kids, but after I went to work, then you went to the bars."

Wife: "I never came home and then left."

Husband: "Sometimes you'd call me on the phone and tell me you'd be home in fifteen minutes, and then you wouldn't be there. You just can't pass those places up."

(Their communication seems reasonably good in that they understand what they are saying to each other and the theme is clear and persistent. I therefore decide on an intervention aimed at what seems to be the prevailing interpersonal transaction.)

Therapist: "Now I think I've listened long enough to jump in here and raise a question with you two. Could you step back from yourselves and answer me this? If you could listen to yourselves, what do you think you would be sounding like?"

Wife: "This is the way it's been going for nine years, back 178 and forth, back and forth. We have sat for hours at a table with a friend, talking back and forth among the three of us, her trying to be the . . ."

Therapist: (interrupting) "But, what do you think you are sounding like?"

Husband: "Kids."

Wife: "Going in circles; it's frustrating to me."

Husband: "Round and round."

Therapist: "What kind of a circle do you think it is? Where are the circles going around and round, being frustrated? What kind do you think it is?"

Wife: "You can call it a love triangle or a vicious circle."

Therapist: "Well, let me reflect back to you what you were sounding like to me—what you were coming through like to me. Now, because it's two men in the room and one woman (addressing both, looking at husband), you were coming through to me a bit parental."

Wife: (interrupting) "Which means . . ."

Therapist: "Just a minute, I'll get to that and spell it out. Now try to think back to the time when you were sixteen or seventeen (continuing to address both, but looking at husband), and you have lost track of time and have come in later than expected. And try to recall what your mother or father might have sounded like at that time: quizzing you, maybe making accusations of where you've been or what you've been doing, like a parent sounding hurt and angry, trying to reason with the teen-ager, trying to get him to shape up, etc., like the parent pointing or shaking his finger at the "bad kid." Now, I shift over here to you (turning to wife), and what do I hear? You sound like a teen-ager trying to deal with a parent who looks to you like he or she is trying to manage you too much, keep too tight a control on you. And you are trying to get loose, and you're sounding a bit defiant—like you're trying to justify yourself, defend yourself, somewhat like a teen-ager put in that spot would naturally do. Like when you said, in effect, "She's my friend, 179 whatever else she is doesn't make any difference. She's my friend." So the more you act the way you act, the more you act the way you act. (Addressing both in turn.) And it goes on as you have said, around and around, over and over, without any end; and nothing ever gets resolved."

(From the typescript alone this may not appear accurate. Missing in the written form are the voice tones, facial expressions, and gestures.)

Wife: "You understand that, John? He's explained exactly how we are in words that I never know how to explain."

Therapist: "It's easier for me to see from where I'm sitting. I'm not caught up in it like you are; and besides, I've seen it so many, many times before. Seeing it is easy. Getting out of it and treating each other in a different way is very, very hard. How long did you people say you've been in it now?"

Wife: "Nine years—to the point that I didn't even want to live anymore. I didn't want us to live together anymore. I thought I'd rather be dead than have another divorce. I've always been a fun-loving person, and—like I tried to explain to him the other night—I feel like I've been nailed to the ground and can't move. I remember when I was younger, my mother, well she really wasn't bad, but she had never gone out on dates and things like that, and I had to be home by a certain time. And if I wasn't, my father would come and find me. But I wasn't nagged. I had a lot of responsibilities, but they didn't nag me."

Therapist: "As I recall the history you told me, the reins were held pretty tightly on you. Didn't you tell me you weren't permitted to go to a drive-in?"

(I attempt to get at the wife's sensitivity to bossiness to help her with it and stimulate empathy in the husband.)

Wife: "Right, they thought I was too young."

Therapist: "Also, that you couldn't dress like the other girls, wear make-up, and couldn't get your hair cut like you wanted—like they were fighting your growing up."

Husband: (interrupting) "Even though you and I went to school together, I don't know what went on at your house, how your parents treated you. I guess just like anybody else, you had this to do and that to do before you could go anywhere."

(Husband responds defensively and destroys my effort to move in the direction of understanding. Perhaps it would have been better for me to have attempted to deal with his defensiveness at this point by blocking out the wife and trying to understand his feelings and where they came from.)

Wife: (addressing Therapist) "One time after John beat me up and I was talking to his sister about his temper, she told me there were many times he would get that mad at his mother, except that he had to hold it in because of what would happen if he ever told her off and his father found out about it. His father told me that if he ever laid his hands on me again, that I should tell him and he'd straighten it out. His mother and I have never been particularly in love with one another, I don't think. I hope that I'm not like that when my kids get up to marrying age and I think that they are marrying beneath them, because it's up to the two people involved; and they get married because they want to get married. I've always had the feeling that John's mother doesn't like some of the things that I do. And in the beginning, when we were first married, John used to call them—his mother and his sister—all the time. And he would tell them what I did wrong, and what I did right. And I've understood this more as I got older, that sometimes mothers think that their kids can't do any wrong. Of course, there are things   *181*

I wouldn't want my son to do. I hope I go about it in the right way."

Therapist: "Hold it, I'm spotting another problem here, or at least something that could be a problem. I'm hearing you talk twice as much as you (turning first to wife and then to husband). Now I would guess that that could mean that you know a great deal more about her than you know about him."

(I decide to try to approach the communicational imbalance and to throw some support to the husband in this previous comment and the next two comments.)

Husband: "Yeah."

Wife: "I've had to pry things out of him."

Therapist: "Yeah, I'm not sure if that's what it is though. He sits and listens and you talk. I wonder if you were a little bit quieter, if he'd come out a little bit more; or if you'd come out a little bit more, she'd be a little quieter. I could tell right from the beginning that it was going to be more difficult to get to know *you* then to get to know *you;* because you come out with things more, and you seem to have difficulty doing that."

Wife: "Well, I know what it can do to somebody to hold things in."

Therapist: "Yes, and I guess you have been to psychiatrists before, haven't you?"

Wife: "Yes, but I wasn't able to speak as freely then as I am now. There were things I didn't want to say to hurt John."

Husband: "Well, if you didn't want to hurt me, why did you do the things you did? The first day after we were married, why did you go out? And what time did you come home?"

Wife: "I don't even remember that. I probably went to

the bowling alley. Maybe I did stay out late, and it wasn't right to do that; but I don't even remember about that."

(My efforts fail and they return to their prevailing interpersonal pattern.)

    Husband: "You said you had been married before and . . ."

    Wife: "Yes, I was married before; and then I got used to having my freedom. And then being married again, I didn't want it to be like it was before."

    Husband: "Was it right at the time? Or were you just thinking of yourself. If I thought of myself all the time, where do you think we would be?"

    Wife: "Well, that depends upon what mood you're in."

    Therapist: "Hey, what are you doing, what are you sounding like?"

    Husband: "Same thing."

    Therapist: "Very good. You can catch yourselves at it now."

(This is more a hope than an actuality. I think I was feeling disappointed about the failure of my prior intervention.)

    Wife: "I have to try to convince him all the time what my thoughts are; all the time I have to convince him."

    Husband: "What do you mean, what your thoughts were?"

    Wife: "Why I did what I did or whatever."

    Husband: "Does that mean that everytime we have an argument, we have to rush out to a night club and talk over our problems with somebody else?"

    Wife: "No, no, no."

    Husband: "Seems to me that that's what you're trying to say."

    Wife: "Every night before I'd go out to bowl, you'd start 183 a big argument and I left the house a nervous wreck. Sometimes I was such a nervous wreck that I couldn't even bowl."

Husband: "You can't say all the time."

Wife: "No, I'm not saying all the time—some of the time. But you're going back a few years, aren't you?"

Husband: "I was still working a few years ago, and you didn't stay around the house then."

Therapist: "Hey, you two don't have to go back three years, eight years, or even three days, you're doing it right now. You (addressing the wife) seem to be feeling like you have to justify yourself, defend yourself; and you (addressing the husband) seem like you have to get command of her, get her to obey you right now."

Wife: "I feel like he dominates me too much; I feel like I'm in a Nazi prison camp—Hitler rule or something like that."

(They incorporate my explanation into their argument and use it against each other. It fails to soften their defensiveness.)

Husband: "But that's what I told you what I feel like. Every time when I come home and it's payday, the check has to be there or there's hell to pay. And you know it as well as I do."

Wife: "What do you want to do with the money? Isn't the money to pay our bills?"

Husband: "Sure. And if the bills don't get paid, then I ask you, where did this go, where did that go."

Wife: (overriding) "And I write it all down for you. I have to account for every penny."

Husband: "Yeah. But why should I have to come home every week, every payday, and give you the check?"

Wife: "I told you, you don't have to give it to me."

Husband: "Yeah, you did. But what did you say after that?"

Wife: "I said that I could earn my own money."

Husband: "Just like you've been saying lately, the money that comes into the house that you earn is your money."

Therapist: "That's interesting. That looks to me like you've just switched roles. Now you're (addressing husband) sounding like the teen-ager who has a job and has to turn over all of his money to what looks like to him a strict parent. And you're (addressing wife) sounding like the parent who has to be very responsible and handle the money. So, it looks to me like you've switched places, switched roles. Do you do that often?"

(In retrospect I would have to say that this is inaccurate. Frustration led me into error. This demonstrates the value of listening to taped interviews for self-supervision.)

Wife: "I usually handle the money because he doesn't like to."

Therapist: "Yeah, but did it sound to you like you switched roles, like it did to me—like he took your place just then, and he took yours?"

More of the same.

Wife: "When I was a child, I used to get a dollar allowance. But then, when I got to be around eleven or twelve, I started earning my own money by babysitting. Then, if I wanted a pair of hundred-dollar roller skates, I worked, saved my money, and bought them for myself. And I worked in a dry cleaners at fourteen and in a restaurant at sixteen. And I've always been what you might call independent with responsibilities. I can't walk away from a responsibility or a job I take on right today."

185

Husband: "Most kids then that you ran around with did work. All kids worked in those days."

Wife: "How would you know? When I was eleven or twelve you didn't even know me!"

Wife: (addressing Therapist) "John tells me I don't work around the house, I don't bring any of the money in, and everything in that house is his; he's worked for it and earned it, and none of it is mine."

Therapist: (interrupting) "Now we've only got a couple of minutes left before the end of the session, and I'm wondering what you both think about what went on here today."

(This represents an effort to end on at least a neutral, if not a positive, note. It is also an effort to get the couple to a different level, one of thinking and talking about their immediate experience.)

Wife: "I do all the talking; he only answers to what I bring out. He asked you a question."

Therapist: "I asked the question of both of you."

Wife: "I don't want to be the only one to answer; I'm too mouthy."

Husband: "I can't be an optimist. It's like it always is with us. We argue back and forth, and then we stop and walk away from each other. And then everything is just the same."

(An accurate summary of what has occurred in the interview and continues to occur throughout the short therapy.)

Wife: "Don't you feel more comfortable arguing in front of an outsider, somebody who doesn't know much about either of us?"

(Her only attempt to be reassuring and positive. The sword in this comment is also evident.)

186

Husband: "I'm not the one who is used to going and consulting others about my problems—you are. Or even if you want to do something, instead of asking me, you go ask someone else."

Wife: "No."

Husband: "Why you can't say you don't."

Wife: "That depends upon what you're talking about."

Husband: "Just about anything."

Wife: "No."

Therapist: (interrupting and addressing the husband) "What you just said about Mary talking to other people about her problems, that's not such an unusual thing. You know, we men have a much more difficult time talking about our problems with others than women do. Often it's okay for them, but not okay for us."

Husband: "I'd rather talk to my wife about my problems than to anyone else—any of my friends."

Wife: "There's another thing that explains it. People of (husband's nationality) usually talk only to a small group of people, mostly their family and very, very close friends. That's a trait."

Therapist: "One of the points I was trying to make . . ."

Wife: (interrupting) "He come from a very close-knit family, so sometimes it's been family, family, family."

Therapist: (continuing) "Hold it, the point I was trying to make here was the difference between men and women in seeking help. It may well be more difficult for John to come seeking help than it is for you because of that."

(Another supportive comment for the husband. I judged him to be the more vulnerable and, at this point, less motivated for therapy.)

Husband: "Yes, it is more difficult for me than it is for her."

Therapist: "Well, now that you've experienced it a little bit, how is it feeling?"

Husband: "Well, it is better talking to someone who knows something than to my friends, because their arguments are probably the same; and they probably do the same thing and give me bad advice."

Wife: "And they couldn't have possibly have listened to all the people that this man has."

Husband: "They haven't got the knowledge."

Wife: "Sure."

(They do end on a somewhat positive note, but this is transitory.)

Therapist: "Okay, we have to stop for today. This will be your regular hour for as long as you need it, and we'll meet again next week at the same time."

Interview 4

This verbatim interview is included because the couple involved were near the end of the second phase of therapy or in the early stage of the third and final phase of therapy. Note the difference between my activity in the first three interviews and this one. Most of my interventions are more "analytical." During this session I was feeling that I could count on the couple not to get too far off the track—in a communicational sense—to be able to bring themselves back. They also seemed to me to be confronting each other more in adult-to-adult terms than they had in earlier treatment sessions. They do not fall too deeply into blaming and accusing and are more oriented toward an effort to reach understandings of each other. I did not teach the husband the psycho-analytic language he is wont to use: "compensate for" or "inferiority complex." Prior to entering conjoint marital therapy and following his second divorce he had had about two years of intensive analytically oriented psychotherapy with another therapist.

Because the husband is a prominent person in his community and even has a national reputation in his field I have drastically changed many of his comments about his work. Also he is an immigrant, and, while he speaks English in a way that is clear to an intelligent American, his syntax is such that his nationality might be identified without my revisions.

Therapist: "Okay, the tape is on."

Wife: "Why don't you begin today?"

Husband: "I don't have anything."

Wife: "You must have something."

Husband: "No, nothing."

Wife: "Okay, then I'll begin. It seems to me that sometimes you answer me in a loud tone of voice when I talk to you a certain way. You don't like it, but it seems to me that lately you have been very abrupt and curt, almost to the point of being rude to me. I haven't said anything about it, but it has been bothering me. I'm just wondering if you have some kind of a feeling inside that makes you talk to me in that voice. Do you realize it when you are doing it?"

Husband: (mumbles).

Therapist: "How's that?"

Husband: "Could you give me an example?"

Wife: "I can't think of anything specific. I mean, usually it's if I ask you a question or something, and you answer me in a very short, curt, abrupt way. And you have a look on your face like, 'I don't want to be bothered'."

Husband: "Can you give me an example?"

Wife: "I can't think of a specific example, but it has happened. I can't think of exactly what I said to you at a certain time."

189

Husband: "Give me an incidence."

Wife: "I can't think of something specific. It's happened many, many times. I can't think of exactly what I said to you."

Husband: "Well, then my position is that maybe this is imaginary."

Wife: "Well, perhaps it is imaginary, but . . ."

Husband: (interrupting) "I can give you an example."

Wife: "Okay, then give me an example, as apparently you know what I'm talking about." (Husband and wife both laugh softly.)

Husband: "Mary has a habit . . . As soon as I come home—and it's really getting now to be that I go to sleep at ten , . . I get up at six-thirty or so, because the last few weeks I've had early business meetings. I'm very busy during the daytime, so that at night after supper, I just go to sleep on the couch. Mary has a habit of—as soon as I come home, say around five-thirty—talking to me about all kinds of things. That's the time I'm not in the mood to talk to anyone about anything, especially about the house, the neighbors, or something like that. And I think that's the time she means. One thing I have a habit of, you see, I have a definite pattern . . ."

Therapist: "You sound like you're telling me about it instead of explaining it to Mary."

(Because the husband was so used to individual therapy, it was necessary for me to remind him frequently that I wished him to address his wife.)

Husband: "Well, okay (laughs), let me turn this way. (Turns to face wife.) So, I have a habit that's really a pattern—it's practically every day that I do it that way—at least on workdays, I come home about five-thirty or six o'clock, the first thing I want to do is look at my mail. Sometimes I get irritated about the mail, because the mail is left in all kinds of places—sometimes the kitchen, sometimes the living room, sometimes the desk—and I don't like to have to look around for it. I like it to be in one place, so I can find it, look at it. So I get irritated about this—sometimes, not all the time, because it is usually the kitchen, so I start looking in the kitchen. But in the kitchen it could be by the sink, by the refrigerator, or somewhere else, so I still have to look around. Sometimes it is in the dining room. So I have a habit of reading the mail. The second thing, I have a habit of reading *The Wall Street Journal*. I read it regularly; I look for articles relating to my business. Then I go to my bedroom; I take off my tie, shoes, and jacket, put on my slippers and go to the couch. I sit on the couch, start reading the newspaper. Before I read the newspaper, I make a martini. I read the newspaper and drink my martini. Now at that time I'm not interested in anything about the house, a broken window, or sometimes, for example, you call me at the office for a discussion because Ricky broke a window. Now what the hell can I do! He broke a window; he got into a temper. So he got into a temper. You have a temper; I have a temper; so does he. And everybody is entitled to break a window at least once a year—not more than once a year, because it costs money. So that's it. But, you see, as soon as I enter, she has a few things for me. And the question is coming up, 'Who calls whom at the office,' because she has certain items to discuss. Well, sometimes she calls me and I'm very short, quick, abrupt—I'm very busy. Well, then I'm supposed to call. I forget to call sometimes, but generally I call. Now, you really have to understand . . . In other words, when I'm in my office I say, 'I can't talk now, I'm busy' or 'I'll call you back.' And I usually write a note for myself to call. When I'm busy, what am I supposed to do? I have things that must be done before I leave the office. So what if I 191 forget sometimes and don't make the conversations long, because I don't have the time. Just tell me what it is you want. If I have time, fine, I'll talk. I have executives coming in and out of my office . . ."

Wife: "Well, this is why I don't want to call you at the office . . ."

Husband: (interrupting) "No, that's okay . . ."

Wife: (continuing) "Well, this is why I asked you just to call me at the end of the day, just before you leave to go home . . ."

Husband: (simultaneously) "There is no harm in calling . . ."

Wife: (continuing) "And that way I think it would solve the problem about my calling. I don't like to call you at the office."

Husband: "But I can't make a note for myself every day to call, which I usually do most of the time. There's no harm in calling, unless I say I'm busy. Don't go through a long conversation if you realize I'm busy. I'm busy, and sometimes I say so abruptly. After all, I'm not being paid to talk to my wife on the phone, I'm there for other purposes. You can call, but don't tell me about Rick breaking a window, all the bad news and how much it costs—that's of no concern to me. You can handle that. He broke a window; it just has to be replaced. You go ahead and replace it. And when I come home, don't bother me right away. I want to take off my shoes, read my newspaper, have my martini. This is my entertainment, Mary, I don't have many entertainments, I mean, I don't play golf . . ."

Wife: "But, but then we never sit down and talk to each other, because the time you come home, you sit, read your newspaper, fix your martini, go back to the paper, see what's on television. Then we eat supper, I'm cleaning up the kitchen, I have to give Ricky his bath and get him ready for bed. By the time he's in bed, it's time for you to go to bed. You've been going to bed at ten o'clock . . ."

Husband: (interrupts) "That's not fair. I haven't had any time off for a vacation and physically I'm tired."

Wife: (continuing) "I need someone to talk to at the end of the day. I mean, I'm relating to a child all day, and, you know, it's kind of nice to be able to sit down and talk to an adult at the end of the day."

Husband: "Well, I try to talk to you. I fall asleep on the couch, and I know that's terrible. And then we go through something like this stupid call I got. I was sleeping, and about midnight Mr. Smith called me and was very upset about some company situation. He was very upset; he was very concerned. I mean, he wasn't being abusive or pressuring me, he just wanted to discuss it. He apologized for waking me, but what the heck, I get physically tired. In the work I do, I have to use my mind. I'm not supposed to lose my temper; I'm supposed to smile, develop good relations and friendships with people. It's not fair to ask a man to do more than he is physically able. So maybe when we are financially in better shape, we can go away for a month. I'm dying to get a whole month. There's a pile of books which I'd love to read—not think about the office, daily routines. It's not that I don't want to talk to you, you have to realize human limitations. What shall I do—give up my job? That's one way, and if it will make our marriage better, then I will. In due time I'll cut down my work load and responsibilities at the company, and in a year . . ."

Wife: "Oh, I don't want you to give up your work; that's the last thing I want . . ."

Husband: "We can't have it both ways. So I think that's going to happen, and I'm glad. I go to bed early, because I get up refreshed. Look at me today. If I would have sat down and talked to you till one o'clock or something like *193* this . . . I know you want me to stay with you while you watch TV, but that can be till one-thirty . . ."

Wife: (interrupting) "When?"

Husband: "Well, one night you said, "why don't you stay up longer?" And it was about midnight."

Wife: "Oh! When?"

Husband: "About two weeks ago. I think you should be pleased that I go to sleep early because of this—because physically it puts me in a better position to do my work."

Therapist: "Okay, it's clear that you understand Mary's need to talk, that you would like to talk to her. But it's also clear that you are depleted, that you 'circuits' are overloaded; you don't have enough energy left to do it. But, that leaves a vacuum for Mary, who . . . As she stated very nicely in her own words, she's been with a kid all day; she hasn't had an adult to talk with, to get her feelings out. And I don't think this business of the window is so important. I think she just needs to talk about something, something that comes along, even a little thing. And it's a compliment that *you* are the adult who is most important for her to wish to talk with."

(Husband and wife interrupt simultaneously. Wife gets the floor.)

(In this comment I attempt to be empathic with the competing needs of both.)

Wife: "Well, to me at the time, the broken window wasn't such a little thing. Let me explain. I was getting ready to go to work that day, and I had taken Ricky outside for a while. I picked up the mail, and it was time for me to go in and start getting ready for work, and he didn't want to come in. I picked him up and carried him in and put him down by the door. And he proceeded to have a temper tantrum and he put his foot through a glass windowpane in the door. To me, this was a major crisis (laughs). I was rushed. It was two o'clock. I had to be at work at two-thirty. I hadn't even started getting ready for work, and just at that moment it was a major crisis to me: what are we going to do? We have to get this glass repaired, and I called a glass company to find out what it was going to cost. I called John, and he said, 'We'll take care of it later.' And he just brushed me off . . ."

Husband: "I had two people in my office."

Wife: "I realize that. But at that point, I think it's a little unfair of you to say, 'You shouldn't bother me with these trivial things.' Because to me at that point, it wasn't really a trivial thing. I mean it was . . ."

Husband: "I know, you were worried about the bill. They told you that it would cost forty to fifty dollars. I appreciate it. I am trying to say that I understand. I do try to talk to you sometimes, but she only reads some parts of the newspaper. What is it? The funnies, the society page—and I read the whole thing.

Wife: (laughing) "I start with the women's page, then the editorial, and then the funnies."

Husband: "And I am more interested in the news and read it in detail. But sometimes I try to talk with you, and you are reading the newspapers.

Wife: "So you interrupt me when I am reading something important to me.

Husband: "But I do want to talk with you. Just give me time. I have gotten myself overloaded at work right now and come home dead tired. And then I like to spend a little time playing with the boy. We do discuss things, Mary. It is not as bad as you say it is. You also exaggerate things. Well, I do the same thing. You exaggerate things like about the window. So the window is broke; it is broke. What can you do? Have it replaced and pay for it. I will put a piece of cardboard in until they fix it.

Therapist: "Again, let me say, or rather let me raise the question in a different way this time. As I understand it, Mary works two half-days per week, but the majority of her time is spent in isolation with housework, child care, etc. So, where is she to take her need for adult companionship, since you are clearly—and this is understandable—overburdened and at the present time unable to meet her need for adult companionship and someone to lean on?"

(The husband has seemed to me to be overfocused on his needs. I decide to highlight the wife's needs.)

Husband: "I agree with you. She doesn't have anyone. I have my people at work with whom I can at least satisfy my intellectual needs. My work is very challenging, and I do get a lot of help from some people. I do get a lot of cooperation from them, but I have to do things right and be very careful with people to keep them happy and cooperating. They like to work less and get paid more, and I have to push them real hard but do it in a tactful way. You should see the work assignments I have to get done some way. The previous director of my division was somewhat lackadaisical. And I have already increased the work assignments from one page to two, and it really ought to be increased to three. So it is very difficult for me to put them to work doing what they should have been doing all along and not arouse their antagonism toward me. So all of these things take energy; my mind is always thinking about ways to make our operation more efficient. And also I am writing that book about managerial practices, and I have a contract with a publisher. You are really raising another issue. If I keep on like this, I could get more and more involved and have less and less time for Mary—if I keep saying yes to things which I am asked to do. I also have to get that other division in the company to work with us. Before now the two divisions had been like two warring tribes, and I have to be the peacemaker. That is what it amounts to. It is really very difficult, particularly at first, to take over an executive position when the one who was in that position before has let things go to hell. I have to develop new plans, new programs, and at the same time keep in mind the personnel problems, the morale problems, in the division. And I have to raise issues which have never been raised before. So if we fail to show progress and fail to show a profit within a reasonable length of time, the whole thing will fall down on my head. You know about the meeting I had yesterday with the treasurer. That was really a rough one. You know how he pushes everyone around, how he makes enemies—I have told you about that—and then I have to go around cleaning up his messes." (The husband goes on in this vein for some time, talking of his responsibilities and the frustrations which he encounters in attempting to carry them out.)

Therapist: "I guess it is time for me to raise another kind of question with you, Mary, would you trade John in for a man who had a more ordinary job, an eight to five schedule with less responsibility and without the recognition and prestige which goes along with his present job?"

(I know from my individual interviews with the wife and from previous sessions with them that the wife gets a great deal of gratification from her husband's reputation, prestige, ambition, and success.)

Wife: "Of course not."

Therapist: "And let me raise a second question with you. Wasn't his intellect, his drive, his ambition to get ahead the very features which made him interesting and attractive to you in the first place?"

Wife: "Mh, yeah. I agree with you 100 percent. I think 197 so, and I think through John I have grown a great deal intellectually."

Husband: "Sometimes we have to pay prices for our gains one way or the other, you know."

Wife: "I certainly don't think that I could relate to a man who is not intelligent and who was not ambitious. And I want to make another point here that is on the positive side. I think that when we first started coming here, we were both so hostile. Between four and five o'clock, when I was thinking about John coming home, I used to get all upset and my stomach was tied into knots. I would get tired and depressed, and I used to just dread seeing his car pull up in front. I used to dread seeing you come home. And now gradually my whole attitude has changed; and now I watch for you and look for you, and I really enjoy having you come home. I think this is a very positive indication that we are working things out, so I look forward to it. And then you sit down and don't seem to want to talk with me."

Therapist: "I hope you are aware of the degree to which you are being complimented."

(I wish to emphasize the positive in what the wife has said and deflect the husband from responding to the last part of her last sentence.)

Husband: (jocularly) "Yes, that's nice. Another point which I would like to bring out, Mary, is that it is going to get worse before it gets better. If I don't show those characters success—and to these guys success is money—they will fire me. Either I move this division ahead, or there is no place there for me as its director. And before I would let them fire me, if I saw it coming, I would resign. And if I succeed—and this worries me and bothers me too—I wonder where that will lead. It bothers me that it may lead to my having to do more and more, that I will be given additional responsibilities that I don't really want. So I am going to have to watch it and learn how to say no when they start dumping more things on me. But I want to say again that it is not that I don't want to talk to you when I come home. It is just that I need some time to rest and pull myself together.

Wife: (interrupting) "May I bring up another incident that upset me and made me mad. The other night, just before going to bed and eating your watermelon . . . (Turning to Therapist.) When it is in season he eats a lot of watermelon; he loves it."

Husband: (interrupting) "You mean when I threw those seeds on the floor—awh—awh, I was just teasing you."

Wife: "No, no, I don't think so entirely. I think there was some hostility in that."

Husband: "No, no."

Wife: "Well, I knew you were joking. But it seemed to me I sensed that there was some hostility too, and I was so mad because I had just cleaned the kitchen that day."

Husband: "That was a childish behavior I know. But I am entitled to be childish sometimes, I am entitled to act like Ricky sometimes."

Wife: (laughs)

Husband: (continuing) "There wasn't any hostility in it. It wasn't because of anything you had done; and then when I saw that you were mad, I cleaned it myself.

Wife: "Okay."

Husband: "I like to have fun with you. I like to joke with you and be a child or be childlike sometimes. If I can't do that in my own home, then where could I act that way?"

Therapist: "Okay, we all need to be little boys with our wives or little girls with our husbands sometimes."

(This gives them permission for healthy regression, which can be fun, and also minimizes any hostility there may have been in his action.)

Husband: "Yes. And more than that, we need to get away from the serious everyday grind more often. And that brings up the question of your mother. She was very nice on the phone the other night, inviting us to come to Florida and spend the holidays with them this year. You know—and I have tried to tell you—that I have an emotional attachment to your parents. And you were surprised to hear me say, regardless of my age, that there is a strong lack within me, a strong feeling of missing a mother and a father. You know I have a great need for someone to take the place for me as a father symbol and a mother symbol. But when your mother starts screaming before dinner, you know what kind of a dinner that is going to be for me. I just collapse emotionally."

Therapist: (interrupting) "Before we get too far beyond it, let me raise a question with you. (Addressing husband.) Several times you have mentioned your difficulty in saying no and your fear or expectation that you wouldn't be able to do so; and you would take on more and more responsibility. Have you asked yourself what is it that is driving you to take on more than you really wish to do?

(Here I wish to get him to deal with a core defense and intrapsychic dynamic. His preceding comment about missing a mother and father reminded me of it. My next question is a leading one and succeeds in getting at what I hoped to open up.)

Husband: "Yes, I think I have some general ideas about that."

Therapist: "What ideas do you have about that—that you have to drive yourself so hard and take on so much almost to the point of being Superman?"

Husband: "I will tell you what I think it is. That is a very important question, and I think that it goes back to my childhood. It goes back to my background, especially back to my mother. I have told you (addressing Therapist) some of this when you were asking me about my childhood. But I don't talk much about it. It's a very painful thing for me to talk about. It fills me with anguish. I didn't even tell you all about it. So I haven't talked much about it to Mary. She doesn't know much about that, about my family and what I went through with them. While I always had all kinds of material advantages, it had a very adverse effect on me to wonder why I was not with my mother and my father. The second thing was that I grew up in an upper-class environment. I grew up in an atmosphere in which my aunt and uncle could afford many things. They could afford, with only one child, to give me all of the material advantages. They could afford to give me luxuries. Even as a child I had tailor-made suits, and they could afford to send me to the best schools, private schools. The clothes I wear now, in comparison to what I wore then, are nothing. And in high school I wasn't a particularly good student so I had three or four tutors. Financially, they could always afford the best for me, and I could have afforded to go any place in the world. They could afford whatever university I could qualify to attend. Also, as a young man, I traveled all over the world, wherever I wanted to go. So, since I was an only child in their family—the family of my uncle and aunt—they could afford all of these things for me. But that is where my inferiority complex came from. I could never understand why my mother and father gave me away to be raised by them. Also all of my friends were rich kids, all of the kids in the schools which I attended were rich kids, and I knew that we, that is my aunt and uncle, were not really wealthy. And I knew that our home was not like their home. I knew that my aunt was working, and that is another source of my inferiority complex. My uncle, who was like a father to me, didn't work; and so it was my aunt who gave me all of this money."

Therapist: "John, I am sensing in you and in what you are saying, also, the need for you to bend over backward to be unlike your uncle."

(Here I felt that talking with him in terms of his need to be unlike his uncle was more acceptable than pointing to his identification with his aunt. Note how the wife joins me and takes over a therapeutic function.)

Husband: "Exactly, that is another possibility. Yes that's true, that's true. That explains why I react so strongly. My uncle just took the money that my aunt gave him like an allowance. My aunt ran that little business all by herself and made pretty good money at it. She was very successful and a very competent woman. Yes, you are right. It looks like I am more like my aunt. I think I see what you are trying to say to me—that I am trying to compensate by being the opposite of my uncle. And when it comes to my son, I am the opposite of my natural father. I am afraid that that is true. I can see that. And another reason for my drive . . . Since I have come to this country, I have felt pushed around because I am a foreigner. So I have to work harder to prove myself, to prove that I can do as well as a native-born citizen. This way they will accept you."

Wife: "You're making a very good point there. You are saying that because you are foreign–born, a "foreigner" in this country, you have to work harder and be better than the average American that you are working with. And I also think that you were brought up by a very domineering aunt who probably put you down a lot in your childhood, and I think you are compensating for this also."

Husband: "She still does that."

Wife: "Yes, I could see that when we visited there last summer.

Husband: "Yes she puts me down and makes me feel

guilty. I even hate to read her letters at all. I dread to read again about the money issues. She does exactly what she wants, and she used to beat me up when I went places she didn't want me to go. Yes, she used to punish me; my uncle never did. She was the strong one, and she was much stronger than what you saw. Can you imagine her thirty years ago?"

Therapist: "So maybe part of it is that you are still fighting your aunt, and you have to be Superman to beat her."

(Interpreting another factor in his defense of a need for power and his work addiction. In this session the husband is more in the "patient" role than is the wife.)

Husband: "Yes, sometimes she really put me on a spot and made me feel very weak and small."

Wife: "You and your aunt are very much alike even in physical appearance, except she is so much shorter, but your facial expressions are practically a replica of hers—also your stubbornness and your drive. All of that shows in your facial expression. It is like looking at her face. Looking at your face is often exactly like looking at her face."

Therapist: "That is another factor. It's like he had to learn to fight fire with fire."

(The wife points to the identification with the aunt before I do. When he seems to take it all right, I endorse this interpretation.)

Wife: "Yeah."

Husband: (laughing) "That is a good point. I never thought about it quite like that. Another thing—my aunt is very tight with money. But in that respect I am completely the opposite. I go to the store and buy all kinds of things, even things we don't really need."

Wife: (laughing) "Yes, your aunt would go to the store

and buy exactly what was needed for dinner, almost counting down to the last pea."

Husband: (laughing) "You remember how much meat we got for dinner. Plenty of starch but no meat. The meat cost too much even to serve to guests. But I am completely the opposite, and so is Mary. Sometimes I even think you are a little wasteful, you cook too much."

Therapist: "I think it is time we get back to Mary's part of it. The point that I made earlier, but would like to make again to you, is that you seem to have picked a man who is the opposite of your father. Now maybe you overshot the mark to some degree, but you seem to have picked someone opposite to your father in many of his traits. And now you are hurting because you don't have enough of him."

(Explaining one of the dynamics of the wife's mate choice and the consequences she was not anticipating.)

Husband: "Yes, and I picked a woman the opposite of my aunt. Huh, am I correct?"

Therapist: "I think so."

Husband: "She is stubborn but otherwise . . ."

Wife: (interrupting) And John is really much more like my mother than my father. They are somewhat similar in personality. You both have very fiery tempers."

Husband: "Okay, but let's go back to Dr. Fitzgerald's last point. What do we do from here (relatively long pause) to sort of balance this (pause)? And I know he is going to leave it to us." (Husband and wife both laugh.)

Therapist: "Right. That is a very good question, and I think once having asked yourself the question, you will soon come upon an answer."

(Here I offer praise for independent thinking and encourage more of it.)

Wife: "Well, I think we have already started to balance the situation without even realizing it. I think that once you understand the problems, you go about your daily lives differently—once you understand things better without thinking I am going to behave in such and such a way. I feel that I have just sort of started to change at least a little bit since coming here, because I understand myself a little bit more. And I think you understand yourself more."

Husband: "Well, try to talk to me, try to tell me what I can do better; and I will try. I really don't want to make things worse for us, even though things may get worse for me at work."

Therapist: "Okay, so see you then next week. Our time is up for now."

Interview 5

The verbatim interview that follows was the forty-eighth conjoint session for this couple who had been in therapy for a little over one year. They had come to therapy after fifteen years of marriage; for about ten of these they had been in a moderate degree of conflict. The wife resented her husband's closeness to his parents and what seemed to her his lack of respect for her. She experienced him as critical, cold, and uncommunicative. The husband, on the other hand, minimized their problems and felt that they could work them out for themselves given more time. He was, however, receptive to trying therapy. They fought bitterly about the way each disciplined their children, especially their teen-age daughter; the wife tended to be overly permissive (according to the husband), while the husband complained about his wife's irritability and nastiness toward him, and he linked this to the days preceding menstruation. The wife had never experienced orgasm, but this had not been viewed 205 as a "problem" until both read a popular sex book. Indeed, this was the event that triggered their decision to seek therapy. The wife consulted her gynecologist, and he referred them to me for marriage therapy. They came already prepared by her physician for conjoint therapy.

Mr. B. was reared on a farm in an emotionally austere atmosphere. His father was dominant, and no one, least of all his mother, could question his authority and get away with it. Angry feelings were freely expressed by the father; socialization of the children was accomplished through criticism, and praise was rarely utilized. His mother was softer with the children when they were very young, but this was forbidden later on.

Mrs. B. was reared in a small rural community and was the youngest child and only girl; there were four old brothers. All of the power in the family seemed to be in the hands of the males.

On her own initiative the patient brought in several pictures of her family of origin; these told a dramatic story better than it could have been described in many words. The patient and her mother, in their facial expressions, body postures, and positioning in the photographs, appeared cowed, frightened, and excluded. Father and brothers looked arrogant, defensively pseudoaggressive, and seemed to be looking down their noses at the women. I read subsequently about the therapist's inviting patients to bring family photograph albums to therapy sessions in *The Book of Family Therapy* (Science House, 1972). I am indebted to this patient for teaching me this way of obtaining quick access to certain aspects of family dynamics.

Therapist: "I'm assuming that this is our last session for now. Or have you changed your minds since two weeks

ago?"

Wife: "I don't know if we decided that this would be our last or our second to last. But, anyhow, I don't even know if we have enough to fill up the whole hour today."

Therapist: "Well, I was thinking that if it was definitely to be the last that we could save some time for review, feedback from you and so forth, later on."

Wife: "Well, things have been going well, and I haven't been feeling very troubled, have you?"

Husband: "No, I think we pretty much covered everything that needs to be covered for now. It's okay with me to make this the last session. Is it with you?"

Wife: "Yes."

(They agree to terminate and also agree that they do not have much on their agenda.)

Wife: (addressing Therapist) "I did read *Lady Chatterley's Lover,* and I found it interesting and beautiful, but not very realistic. (Patient laughs and seems a bit embarrassed.) I've been trying to get John to read it, but he won't."

Husband: "You've had it; you've been reading it ever since we got it, so I haven't been able to. But I will."

Wife: "It's helped me pass the couple of days since the kids went back to school. I haven't been alone all day for years and years and years."

Therapist: "You found somethng unrealistic in it?"

(I decide to explore in more depth her reactions to the book.)

Wife: "Yeah, men really aren't that tender. And I don't think women really enjoy being that passive. D. H. Lawrence wants his women to be too passive. And men aren't really like that gamekeeper; they'd be afraid of being called sissy. I wish you'd read it."

207

Husband: "I will."

Wife: "About that passive thing—sometimes it looks good, but I'm still scared of it—like it's something that could be ridiculed. And I know you say that ridicule is in my own head, but it's still there. And some passiveness looks nice, but it's still too scary."

Therapist: "Well, this may sound repetitious, but I'll say it anyway. I think you know where the scared feelings come from, or at least where most of them come from. We've talked about it many times before. But I understand—and I think I've told you that I do—that just talking about something won't make it go away, doesn't make it vanish into thin air. I think maybe at some point you will have to summon up the courage and just let yourself be passive. Give it a try and see what happens—with John's help, of course.

(To support and encourage them to face their fears and put into practice what they have learned.)

Wife: "John somehow doesn't seem involved enough. You seem to be off in your own separate world."

Husband: "I can't understand why you feel that way, because I do feel involved."

Wife: "You seem sort of cold-natured and reserved."

Husband: "Well, that could be a general statement. But I don't think that so far as our sexual relations are concerned I'm cold-natured and reserved."

Wife: (laughing softly at first) "It's not really fair to blame it on you, because you weren't that way before we were married. Then I sort of ruined it for you."

Husband: "No, I think we grew into a situation, and that's what we're now trying to work our way out of."

Husband: "What you're still worried about is if you allowed yourself to be passive in the bedroom then I would treat you that same way when you're out of the bedroom."

Wife: "Yeah, plus the ridicule in my own head. But he said that therapy would go on working afterward. But I hope (laughing) that we're not going to have to wait for fifty years."

(This suggests that she is encountering some anxiety about letting loose of a defense.

Therapist: "Are you waiting?"

(To explore the resistance.)

Wife: "No, but I feel like I'm caught in a trap. Do you feel like you're caught in a trap with me?"

Husband: "I don't think it's all that bad, even if things were to get no better than they are. It's not that bad, and I think we could accept it and live with it. But I still think we have that little carrot hanging out there waiting for us, and it's worth trying for it."

Wife: "Yeah, I've sort of given up though."

Husband: "Well, I don't think we should give up. I don't think you should pressure yourself to the point where you feel pushed, but I don't think you should give up either."

Wife: (after a relatively long pause) "Yeah, it isn't really that bad. I make it sound terrible, don't I?"

Husband: "Yeah, you make it sound worse than it really is."

Wife: "I think originally I wanted to know why we had so many fights and why they were so bitter and why they were so long. Now I think we know that and we don't have fights like that any more. We just have normal ordinary fights."

Husband: "Yeah, we know how to handle those."

Wife: "And, it's nice to know something about analyzing your dreams too. And the kids get along better. I can't think of anything else that's a problem between us, except you **209** say that you can't get interested in world affairs. You sort of have to be born into it, born into a family that's interested in world affairs."

Husband: "It's a lot easier, but I don't think you have to be born into that kind of a family. It's a lot easier if you've been brought up in that kind of an atmosphere."

Therapist: "I agree, that does make it easier. What makes it important to you that John become interested?"

(In retrospect this seems unnecessary and repetitious. We have covered this ground before, and they probably would have done so with no intervention by me.

Wife: "So we can discuss it together."

Husband: "It's important to her because they did it in her family."

Wife: (interrupting and laughing) "You should have been with us to that X company affair, and then you'd know why it's important. You should be there and listen when a group of those technical guys get together. Oh brother! There isn't an intelligent conversation in the whole bunch, no kidding. There's one group of men watching pro football. And then there's another group of people around the punch bowl, and they're all kind of half-polluted. And they're discussing the Olympics, and some of them are crabbing about the state universities being full of Jews—stuff like that. You know, they don't seem to know what's going on; they don't give a hoot. And I don't want him to be like that."

Husband: "What's more remarkable to me, is that when we got there it was about eight o'clock, and I guess the thing started at four o'clock. There was a certain type of people that were gathered around the punch bowl. Then in one room there were a bunch of women who didn't want to be associated with the rest of us. Then in another room there were a bunch of men around the TV. Then out in

210

the yard there were a few couples talking together in a group; and they seemed to be more our type. The funny thing was the people were all separated off into categories or types of people. It was like segregation had taken place in that short a time."

Wife: "None of them seemed to be able to talk about anything that was very important or interesting to us. We just had to sort of fake it and make up conversation, and it was a relief to get out."

Husband: "Yeah."

Wife: "There was one uninhibited wife who was interesting to listen to. Everyone else thinks she's neurotic and odd, but she was a good conversationalist, and we got a good conversation going with her."

Therapist: "Well, common interests certainly do grease the wheels of any relationship. But as we talked about before, in a marriage there is also room for individuality, so that each person can have his own interest as well as shared ones. If you can't come together on one particular common interest, perhaps you can find another one."

(To encourage individuation in some spheres and togetherness in others.)

Wife: "I read somewhere that after being married for a while you need to find something new to share together, and I thought that was good."

Therapist: "Um hum. Well, the atmosphere between you today does seem very calm and friendly. Would this be an appropriate time to bring out into the open for discussion whatever issues may be waiting in the wings? Or do you feel that there aren't any that are that important or that you can deal with them as they come up?"

(I decide to push forward.)

Husband: "I think we pretty much dealt with all of the issues; I don't think there are any skeletons hiding in the closet, do you?"

Wife: "No."

Husband: "There's a problem that keeps coming up that I see; and she doesn't seem to recognize it or realize it when it's happening—and that's about a week before her period is to come."

Wife: "No, it's not always before. It's crazy. Sometimes it's the week after."

Husband: "We've talked about it before, and we know some of the reasons for it. But it's still a problem we have to face monthly."

Wife: "Well, I usually know how to deal with it if I know what the date is, but I lose track sometimes. If I find myself irritable I have to go look at the calendar and check out my cycle and then figure if that's reason enough to be mad, or if there's some other reason. But for some reason, it does seem to come often a week after. I must have some kind of mixed-up hormones."

Husband: "It comes about the time you have that mid-month bleeding, doesn't it?"

Wife: "Well, I'm really not worried about that. I talked with Dr. F. (her gynecologist) about it, and he assured me that it's normal. He said that women don't get together and talk about it, so that some of them think that it's not normal to have it. But I know better than that."

Therapist: "What you're talking about then is the time of ovulation."

Wife: "Well, it's about a week after."

Therapist: "When you say 'a week after,' you mean a week after day one of your period, which would make it day eleven?"

Wife: "No, I mean starting the cycle with the first day of bleeding, it's seven or eight days after that."

Therapist: "Well, then it's preovulatory; it's not exactly the middle of the cycle, and it doesn't seem to be premenstrual."

Husband: "Ovulation is supposed to be on day fourteen, if it's a twenty-eight-day cycle, isn't it?"

Therapist: "Yeah, you could say that, on that day, say plus or minus two or three days. The body doesn't work exactly like a clock, you know. There are individual variations, which doesn't mean, of course, that a person is crazy if they depart somewhat." (Husband and wife both laugh.)

(This and previous comments are designed to further educate and reassure with respect to sexual matters.)

Husband: "Well, we have to watch out for that, but I think we've covered everything, at least everything we know about for now."

Wife: "I can't think of anything either. You said we'd have a review, how do we do it."

Therapist: "Well, something that I would welcome and that could be useful to you as well—if you could today try to get in touch with two or three things that have been meaningful to you that you could pick out . . . pick out two or three things or however many that we learned together that have been meaningful or helpful to you as individuals or as a couple, about yourself or each other."

(Spelling out what I mean by "review.")

Husband: "It's going to be hard to pare it down to two or three (laughing)."

Therapist: "Well, picking out whatever you see as highlights."

Wife: "As we went along, I made a list of things that   213 you did that I liked and that I didn't like, but that's not exactly what you're asking."

Therapist: "Well, I was going to ask for that later."

(Affirming that this is what I mean by "feedback.")

Wife: "Okay (laughing)."

Husband: "Well, do you want to summarize that part of it now?"

Wife: "Well, that's not what he's asking now."

Therapist: "No, first I was asking for what you think you've carried away that has been useful and meaningful to you in terms of understanding."

Wife: "About two thousand things."

Therapist: "Well, I don't think we have time for all those." (Husband and wife both laugh.)

Wife: "One of the most important things to me was when you analyzed my dreams, and you figured out all of those crazy things that were going on in my head."

Husband: "I think one of the most important things was unraveling those things in her background. We could begin there as a starting point. There are several really significant things that have helped us both understand our situation. And one of them was about your sleeping in your parents bedroom, and this helped us understand where one of your attitudes came from. Another thing then—and I don't mean to be dwelling on your problems, but I think it's very important how we understood the impact of your father and brothers on your attitudes and feelings—and one of them was the picture you brought in."

Wife: "Yeah, I forgot about that. I was really scared to bring that picture in. I thought you'd think I was some kind of a nut. But until I brought that picture, it was really hard to talk about my family. You kept asking me about my family, but one of our rules was that we didn't talk to others about what really went on. We were supposed to put on a front and fake it and not talk about how we really felt. So it was really hard for me to talk about my true feelings. We were supposed to look warm and affectionate, but underneath we really weren't. So I hit upon the idea of bringing the picture in, but I didn't think you would know what I meant. But you did right away, so that was a big relief. I had this feeling about psychiatrists, that they were God and perfect and all that. And if you made a big mistake right away, it would have messed things all up. I had to go on for a while feeling that you were what I thought you were, and you caught what I meant in the pictures."

Husband: "There were a couple of later things that came out—I haven't thought about them lately."

Therapist: (Noise of the vacuum sweeper is beginning to sound so loud that we are having a difficult time understanding each other.) "Would you excuse me for a moment, so I can ask my wife not to mess up our tape? (Husband and wife both laugh. "Go ahead." I leave the room and ask my wife to discontinue vacuuming for a few minutes.)

(My office is in my home, and sometimes my wife acts as cleaning woman.)

Husband: "Another we learned about was your premenstrual anticipation of punishment."

Wife: "I seem to have gotten over that—that is, unless I switched it to eight days after. But that is a good one."

Husband: "There is something else that we learned that is very important that I can't get a hold of right now."

Wife: "The explanation of that dream where the child was run over by the car—you know, the castration thing."

Husband: "I think that was important too."

Wife: "If you're walking around with an unconscious mind that doesn't know what sex you are, it's pretty hard to behave 215 right. You know what sex you are; but in your feelings, it just doesn't come out right."

Husband: "One of the things I learned about myself was that I learned from my parents to squelch my feelings, to keep them hidden. And I've had to fight that, bring them out into the open, and be more understanding so that she can understand my feelings."

Wife: "Yeah, and that helps. You act more human."

Husband: (laughs)

Wife: "You don't have to be tough, brave, and all that junk all the time. You could admit that you can be scared, and that's more human."

Husband: "Another thing, a specific thing that was helpful to me, was when we talked about my job pressures, especially during meetings when I used to feel that I had to give instant answers. I learned that it isn't really normal or expected for a person to have to give instant answers without thinking. So now I don't even try to, unless I have the answer. I give myself time to think it over. I learned to let them wait if I don't have an instant answer. And that has relieved a lot of pressure on me."

(The expectations of his inner father have been modified.)

Wife: "Good."

Wife: "There are countless things that I know helped, but I can't think of any more right now."

Husband: "One of the recent things was when you learned that you could be honest with me about your feelings right away."

Wife: "Yeah, I'm supposed to be honest in bed, but . . ."

Husband: "No, not just then, always."

Wife: "Yes, I did and sometimes do hide my feelings for a while. It's hard to be honest with them, even if you're

a woman."

Therapist: "Sure."

Husband: "Yes, you did that to protect yourself from ridicule."

Wife: "Like yesterday. I often feel miserable on Sundays. And instead of just taking it for granted, I tried to think about it and realized there must be a reason; and I just don't have to feel that way. And I think that I really could get a hold of the reason why, if I thought about it and worked with it long enough."

Husband: "I think that probably goes back to Sunday evenings at home, probably during the war, while you were in high school. That was kind of a dull, miserable time for you."

Wife: "Yeah."

Husband: "On Friday and Saturday evenings there was something to do, but in a small town a Sunday evening was kind of dull and miserable."

Wife: "Yes, but I don't really think that was the entire reason. I think that Mom and Dad usually always had an argument on Sunday, because Mom wanted to keep going to church and Dad wouldn't. He was kind of an atheist. So they always had an argument on Sunday, and Sundays always came out miserable (relatively long pause). We learned some pretty important things about you too."

Husband: (jocularly) "The decompression syndrome?"

Wife: "Yes, leave you alone for at least fifteen minutes after you get home. That really helps. If you hadn't explained that and said that I should do that, I wouldn't have been able to let him alone. I would have gone on feeling sorry for myself."

Husband: "Another thing was the agreement we came to to set aside some time to sit down and talk and iron things out."

Wife: "Yes, that's good too. Having a way to tell each other that we need to talk."

Husband: "And having a way to indicate to each other 217

that we think the other one is getting out of line in our relationship with Jane (their teen-age daughter)."

Wife: "No, we haven't even had to use that signal we made up, have we?"

Husband: "No, I think that just having a signal made us aware of the problem, so that we didn't need to use it."

Therapist: "I've forgotten if you told me what signal it was that you agreed upon."

(Previously I had encouraged the use of nonverbal telegraphic communication so that their words would not obscure their meanings.)

Wife: "We were going to touch each other's face if we felt the other one had done something that was . . ."

Husband: "Out of line."

Wife: "Yes."

Husband: "We haven't had to use it."

Wife: "I guess I kind of forgot about it (relatively long pause). There must be lots of other things, but I can't think of them. Oh yes, getting John to admit that his mother had been harsh with him was something I never expected. I never expected that he would admit that she had any faults at all. She was the sacred area in our life, and he actually admitted that she was somewhat harsh with him. And another thing that John did—he criticized my father. For some reason it made me uncomfortable that he got along with him as well as he did. And he actually found some little thing that my father did wrong and crabbed about it. And that made me feel better . . . I don't know why. I know—because my dad isn't sacred any more (during this passage wife is laughing and sounds delighted)."

(Wife's father image has also been modified. Note the insight and empathy they demonstrate in many of the statements they make

about themselves and each other. Much of the time they serve a therapeutic function for each other.)

Therapist: "Yeah."

Wife: "I can't think of anything else."

Husband: "I know there are others, but I can't either."

Wife: (addressing Therapist) "Would you like to see my list of things you did right and wrong?"

Therapist: "Well, I'll tell you what. Yes, I would. But I've got an idea: It might be easier if I would leave the room for about ten minutes and let you go ahead and read the list."

Wife: "Why?"

(This is an example of my having read about a tactic I want to try. I do so inappropriately; this couple do not need it. It falls flat.)

Therapist: "Well, I think you would feel better that way, because you wouldn't have to look at me. And I'll have it on the tape." (Husband and wife both laugh.)

Wife: "You mean you're going to get mad at me like you used to? You going to raise your voice and swear and be a beast?"

Therapist: "No, but would you feel better if I would leave and do it that way?"

Wife: "No, it's okay. Don't leave."

Therapist: "Do you actually have a written list?"

Wife: "Yes."

Husband: (jokingly) "Is it like a credits list?"

Wife: "Some of it sounds stupid now, but this is the way we felt at the time. When I first came in, I was terrified of talking. And when I faced up to that, you said, 'Oh, that's okay. Lots of people have trouble talking at first.' And 219 you didn't think that was important, but it really was. I had to think about that a lot, and that helped. And then once you said, 'If you would look at my face, instead of looking down at the floor, you might find out that I'm even friendly.' And that was nice, that helped me. And you were really careful with John's feelings; you didn't tromp on him like you did on me. And that was nice, because I kind of drug him in here, and it wouldn't have been fair for you to be mean to him like you were to me. And no matter what I said, you didn't act shocked, and that was good. And sometimes, when I said something really terrible, you had a charming way of looking down at the floor. And that was good—that was my little signal that I was having some effect on you."

(I had been quite confronting with the wife, more so with her than with the husband. But she also amplified my actions through her father and brother filters. There seemed no need to go over the latter again.

Therapist: "That's interesting, because I'm not even aware that I do that."

(Acknowledging that it is possible for things to occur outside of my awareness.)

Wife: "Well, I thought it was cute. And you said that I do well in knowing my own feelings, and that was nice. I was always scared of you, but as we went along, when you said some little thing that helped, I always used it—you know—to keep down enough of the fear so that I could go on talking. You know what I mean?"

Therapist: "Um hum."

220   *Wife:* "And you said that you don't use the word 'cure,'

and I thought that was realistic. You know, you don't say that this person is cured."

Husband: "Well, saying 'cure' would imply that it's a static situation. In the human situation, in human relationships, nothing is static; it's always moving and changing. It's dynamic."

Wife: "Yeah, but I was kind of dumb (laughing)."

Therapist: "I like the sound of that past tense."

Wife: "Well, about therapy I would have expected you to want a cure. I thought that you wouldn't feel proper about yourself unless you could check everybody off as cured. And you said that on a scale of zero to ten that I would rate seven or eight. And while I don't really think that's true, but I felt good when you said that. You make it clear to me that when my teen-aged brothers ridiculed women, that got programmed into my head; and it was still in there. I wouldn't have believed that—and I can't remember what you said exactly—but whatever it was, it helped me believe it. That one sounds stupid now. And one time we were talking about—or I was talking about—what I really wanted out of marriage. And you told me to tell John what it was I wanted; and that was that I wanted him to notice what I do with him and the children and get complimented sometimes. And I said that I had given up on that because men weren't really that way. And you said, 'Men can learn.' And I nearly collapsed. And I was surprised that you said that. He still doesn't do that, but that's okay."

Husband: "I think I do. Maybe I'm doing it in ways that aren't obvious to you, and I'll have to change that."

Wife: (returning to her list) "We have already covered the pictures, so I don't have to go into that. I also found that my daughter was right, that before therapy I didn't really listen to people. (Addressing husband) Don't you think that we really learned how to listen?"

Husband: "Yes."

Wife: "That's one thing about psychiatrists, they really listen."

Husband: "And that brings up another important point. If I don't tell her how I feel, essentially she plays her own record back."

Wife: "We still do that sometimes."

Husband: "Yes, we do at times. But at least we've learned to recognize it and look for it now. We have to listen and see if we're listening rather than playing our own records."

Wife: "Yeah, that was important—when you said that when he presents a blank face I run my own movies on it."

Wife: "You did some bad things too. You said that I over-communicate and that made me mad. But now when I think about it, I think that maybe you're right. (Addressing husband) Do I still overcommunicate?"

Husband: "I haven't noticed that lately."

Wife: "Once you smiled in the wrong place, and I could hardly talk for two sessions. We were talking about . . . (Addressing husband) Do you remember that?"

Husband: "Yeah."

Wife: "We were talking about the fact that I slept in my parents' bedroom until I was five or six years old. And I never thought much about that, even though I read Dr. Spock's book, and he advises that you should get them out at about six months. I still didn't connect it to myself. And you said that the child is bound to wake sometime and witness intercourse and think that he's killing her or something like that. You smiled a little, and I really felt miserable. It was like you were making fun of sex or me. I got the feeling of the old ridicule. Maybe you didn't mean it that way, but that's the way it came through. You don't remember that, do you?"

Therapist: "No, I don't recall that. I'm not aware of having done that. But if I did, maybe I was getting in touch with

222

something within myself that aroused feelings that I didn't know about. I wasn't aware of it at the moment."

(Again acknowledging my vulnerability to having feelings of which I am unaware.)

Wife: "Okay. But at the time I thought, 'He's another one of those men who make fun of sex.' That's about all. But I did think you were really crabby at times, really a beast. But that's part of the therapy, I suppose."

Husband: (laughing) "Like the blue-dress incident."

Wife: "Yes. And sometimes when you'd sit there and say, 'you're pissing me off,' I felt like belting you one. (Laughs heartily.) But that's all I can think of. (Addressing husband.) Do you have anything to add? You said that I should say what John did that made me mad, and I was sitting here saying it. And then you got mad at me for doing that, and I got mad at that. Later on at home we talked about it."

Husband: "I thought that you made him mad because you were trading on his professional toes."

Wife: "Yeah, but I'm the patient. I get to say things; I get to have my say. I was trying to get you to do what I wanted you to do, and I really think you should have done it."

Therapist: "I think you were pushing my grandmother button." (Husband and wife both laugh.)

(I was aware that in trying to control me and the interviews she was doing so, and I decide to reveal this.)

Wife: "My goodness, you mean we have a grandmother buttons too?"

Therapist: Well, yes, if we have enough contact with them we do."

Wife: "Some people think that nursing homes are awful **223** and you should take your parents in to live with you. I'd sure hesitate a long time before doing that when I remember some of the ways that my grandmother answered questions that I asked her. So, I'd hesitate to bring our parents in to live with us."

Husband: "I agree with that one. (pause).

Wife: (addressing Therapist) "What did we do wrong?"

Husband: (laughing) "That's not a fair question. That would take two more sessions."

Wife: "Weren't we pretty good patients, really?"

Therapist: "Yes. We've had some rough times together, but that wasn't actually a matter of you doing anything wrong. By definition, there ain't anything you can do wrong here. You just do what you do, and then we deal with it together."

Husband: "That's what we had to learn—how to deal with it."

Therapist: "Right. Now Mary has given me quite a bit of feedback, and I've had some from you. But I'm wondering if there's anymore."

(Attempting to obtain more balance in this interview.)

Husband: "Well, I'm curious about one thing. Several sessions back you said that this was a typical marital conflict, but with a twist. And I'm not sure what you meant by the twist."

Wife: "I think he meant my castration complex."

Husband: "No, I'm not sure that was it. I don't think we were talking about that then."

Therapist: "I can't recall the context of what I had in mind when I said 'with a twist.' Do you remember the context?"

224   *Wife:* "It was before we got to my dreams. And we were

just stumbling along, and I had expected you to have the therapy more planned."

Therapist: "Maybe I was expressing a feeling of being a bit confused myself, confused or twisted. I really can't remember."

(Again acknowledging that I may have said some things that arose from my feelings. They have been turning the tables, and that's fine with me.)

Husband: "Okay, I can't think of any more specific items that we need to discuss right now."

Therapist: "Well, okay, we'll wrap it up for now then. As a parting comment, I would like to reassure you that you have seniority. So that if you need to come back at any time, there won't be as long a wait as at first. There are usually two dangers here. One, that you would get upset and not give yourselves an opportunity—if you get into a snarl—to use the tools that you've learned in therapy and work it out on your own. The other danger is that out of pride or out of expectation that you would be criticized or something if you would return, that you would wait too long. I can't put any figures on it, but it's important that you give yourselves a reasonable length of time to work things out with each other before returning."

(My goal here is to simultaneously support appropriate independence and appropriate dependence.)

Wife: "I feel a little bit scared to try it without you, but we've got to do it sometime."

Therapist: "That little bit of fear is okay, and I wouldn't wish to take it away from you. It may even be helpful in that it will keep you on your toes and alert to signs of trouble. 225

All that remains now is to wish you well and tell you that it's been a real pleasure working with you."

(To support the constructive use of anxiety and end on a positive note.)

Interview 6

This couple, whose fifth conjoint session is recorded here verbatim, entered therapy because of concern about their contentious relationship as well as their worry about the aggressive behavior of their sixteen-year-old son. They described him as a "bully" toward his peers and younger children, including his younger brother; they also said that his teachers were complaining about his loss of temper and telling them off in class. It was this son's increasingly aggressive behavior that was the immediate precipitating event leading to therapy. They came prepared for marriage or family therapy.

Both spouses are college graduates, intelligent, well-read, strong-willed, and opinionated. Mr. S. works as a director of personnel for a large company and has a strong interest in psychology and sociology; he continues to take courses in both at a nearby university. Prior to their marriage Mrs. S. worked as an executive secretary for the president of the same company. Part of the attraction of each for the other were their shared personality characteristics of efficiency and leadership ability. Their communicational difficulties in therapy have never been more serious than demonstrated in this interview.

Mr. S.'s father was, "not a family man." Although he was frequently laid off from his laboring job on the railroad, he spent little time at home. When at home he was strict, impatient, and quick to anger. "He'd blow up at the tiniest things my brother or I would do, like being a couple of minutes late for dinner," said Mr. S. An uncle of Mr. S. was kind to him and encouraged him to get a college education. In speaking of him the patient said, "I could identify with him, but not with my father." Mr. S. described his mother as warm and affectionate; it was necessary for her to work from the time the patient was two or three because of the father's inconsistent income. He and his brother were left in the care of friends and relatives while the mother worked.

Mrs. S. described a tranquil childhood. Her father was, "a very quiet, peaceful man," and she could not recall one argument between her parents. Her mother was the more decisive and was the leader in the family, but this circumstance "never caused any trouble between them." Her mother was the better educated of the two, and the father depended upon her for advice and problem solving. She emphasized the gentle way her father spoke to her mother and the children. Mrs. S. described her mother as a sensitive, loving, and imaginative person, going out of her way to do nice things for the children and others.

I have confined myself in these comments to those aspects of their backgrounds that seem germane to the interview that follows.

Therapist: "So, what's on your minds today?"

Wife: "It's my turn to be quiet today."

Husband: "Some things have been on my mind for the past couple of weeks. Things have been better in terms of our relationship. I don't know in how many different ways but somewhat better (pause). Two things bugged me this past week. I can tell you that ah (pause) . . .

Therapist: "Before you go on to that, could you be more specific about what seems better, so that we can have a clear idea about those things.

227

(I like to encourage the elaboration of the positive before the patient goes into the negatives in order to soften the blow of the latter.)

Husband: "Sure. I have often thought that we didn't eat very well and that you were a much better cook than that."

(Conflicts around food suggest early maternal deprivation and resultant hostility. (It would be premature to explore this at this time.) There may be a realistic element in this, however, as well as a transference one; the spouse may be depriving her mate of gratifications that are important to him in a "tit-for-tat" transaction.)

Wife: "But, honey, I don't remember you ever saying that."

Husband: "But I did. Don't you remember that I even gave you a list with things that I like on it. It was headed by baked beans and also different kinds of meats, certain kinds of roasts."

Wife: "But I was interpreting what you just said to have to do with quality."

Husband: "I mean both quality and the kinds of meals you prepare."

Wife: "Do you think I am a good cook?"

Husband: "I think so, but there were many times you didn't measure up to what I thought you could do. But during the past couple of weeks we have had some really outstanding meals, and, uh, I really appreciate that. Uh (pause) . . . One thing that bugged me this week was again at the dinner table when you interfered with me when I was reprimanding Jim (their oldest son). You said, "John," when I was angry with Jim for only a minute or two minutes. And I thought that that was inappropriate. Tom was still at the table, and I was angry with Jim for something for just one or two minutes. And you tried to stop me by saying, "John." And I don't like to be interfered with, and, as I have pointed out to you, when I have heard you and Ted (their younger son) get into it when you were angry with him, I sat there and didn't say a word. Sometimes I think you are right, and sometimes I don't even know what it is all about. But anyway I say nothing. I leave it to you and him to work out, and I think you should do the same thing. It's between Jim and me. And if I am angry with him, I have a right to ventilate my feelings, just like you have with yours. The second thing was that, when I came home last evening, you said that you had given my blackboard to Mrs. Smith to use in her dance class. And this upset me because we sat right here, and I told you that it upset me when you gave away two of my books and that I was unhappy when you gave away a couple of my old hats. You said right here that you wouldn't ever do that again. Then, when I came home last night, you say you had given Mrs. Smith my blackboard."

Wife, "But when I gave away those books, that was eight years ago."

Husband: "I don't care how long ago it was. It's an old, well-made slate blackboard. It was given to me as a going-away present when I was transferred here, and you know that I use it when I conduct training meetings at home. I used to use it frequently when we lived in Chicago, but I haven't yet had occasion to use it here. You know that it is my blackboard. I may have an occasion to use it and I may not, but that is unimportant. And you gave it to her without asking me, which would have been the simplest thing in the world. And that really upset me."

Wife: "There is no problem."

Husband: "But, honey, there is a problem. When you give away my blackboard without consulting me, that is a problem."

Wife: "Well, there is a problem here. It was not clearly in mind that it was your blackboard and . . ."

Husband: (interrupting) "But, honey, I don't see how you could regard it as anything other than my blackboard. It was given to me. I put it in a carton and brought it here when we moved."

Wife: "But you haven't used it for three years."

Husband: "That's true. But when we lived in Chicago, on my other job, I used it frequently for every meeting that I held in our house."

Wife: "But you haven't used it yourself in all that time."

Husband: "Right, since we have been here."

Wife: "You have given it over to the children, and they have been using it."

Husband: "I didn't give it over to them. I kept it in the basement and let them use it whenever they wanted to."

Wife: "But there is no problem. I can tell Mrs. Smith that you are going to have a seminar to use it perhaps in March—you will know by then—and if you have use for it I will get it back. Perhaps it would be okay with you if she would use it until then."

Husband: "But that's not the problem. That isn't what bothers me. What disturbs me is that you offer something which clearly was mine."

Wife: "What can I say? The children used it for three years and then, when we moved, it sat in the Jones' garage for six months. And for three weeks I have been hearing Mrs. Smith say, "If only I had a blackboard, I could show the kids this or that." She said it several times, and I felt that if we could help uh . . ."

Husband: (interrupting) "Why couldn't you ask me?"

Wife: "Well, I am sorry."

Husband: "Honey, but if only you would have said that last night. But you didn't."

Wife: "Honey, you shut me off last night."

Husband: "But I did not. You turned around and walked
230 out."

Therapist: (Hand signaling stop. Looking at and addressing wife.) "Let's us take a look at your side of this, Mary. It's sounding to me like instead of being able to take a look at what you are doing, you are instead mainly justifying what you have done. And what's going on right now is much more important than whatever it was that happened last night. If you need to go ahead and act without consulting him about these kind of matters—and he has made it clear that he likes to be consulted, and we will probably have to take a look at that too—then there must be some very good reason or reasons that you keep on doing it. I think I may know why. It sounds to me like you do it kind of automatically, without even having the thought in your head first. This is something that I should consult with John about."

(In this comment I attempt to get through the defensiveness manifested by her self-justification by suggesting that there are other, unconscious and undeliberate, reasons for her behavior. This will simultaneously diminish the husband's hostility, not necessarily immediately but eventually.)

Wife: I will be honest with you. I do not think. I did not think of asking for his permission or his opinion. I didn't. To me, it was the children's blackboard just sitting there not being used, and someone could make some good use of it. But I did not think to consult him (pause). Does a wife have to consult her husband about everything? Or can she have freedom to make some decisions?"

Therapist: "Well, let's approach it from another angle. Supposing that your taste with respect to salt was different from his—that he liked just a little salt and you liked a lot. Would you then continue salting his food more than he wished?" 231

((Since the wife continues to be defensive, although apparently less so, I try again.)

Wife: "No, but it is not that simple."

Therapist: "Well, maybe it really is that simple. It's sounding to me like your expectation is . . . Without even thinking about it, it's a kind of automatic thing—that there isn't any need to consult and you must have learned that expectation somewhere. (Turning to husband.) Where do you think she learned it?"

(I allude to her behavior as representing a learned expectation. What I have in mind is her marriage model, where her mother took for granted that she was the decision maker and her husband welcomed this. I invite the husband to participate in the therapeutic exploration.)

Husband: "I don't know for sure."

Therapist: "Well, could you guess?"

Husband: "I think, but I am not sure, that in your family your mother made most of the decisions, and your father didn't really have very much to say. I think that, but I am not really sure."

Wife: "That's true. My mother did that. But my father did have opinions, and she respected him and respected his views. And he sometimes stated them, but mainly they worked as a team. They still do, but she was the leader of the family."

Therapist: "That is exactly what I had in mind. (Turning to wife.) That is what would come naturally to you. That's what you would do naturally, automatically without thinking, because it is so much a part of you through identification, through imitation, of your mother whom you admired."

(I spell out the identification with her mother in as gentle a manner as possible so as not to arouse more defensiveness.)

Wife: "Yes, I understand that. And that comes as no surprise to me. But can't there be some way that a wife can make some decisions, not the big ones, not the crucial ones, on her own and that the husband would have the same right."

Therapist: "Sure, and I think that is what you two need to work out together, to establish policies on this so that you don't confront each issue *ad hoc.*"

(I encourage couples to negotiate about policies that can avoid conflicts about specific issues in the future.)

Wife: "That would be very helpful, but we haven't been able to do that. Just recently I said to you, 'As soon as we complete our decorating (the family has recently moved into a new home), we should think about having some dinner parties. We owe a lot of people, and it's time for us to be meeting our social responsibilities.' And you leaned back in your chair and laughed and mocked me and made me feel ashamed. And I was not issuing orders or making decisions, I was only trying to talk it over with you."

Husband: "I don't understand what you are saying."

Wife: "What I am trying to say, what I said, that when I said to you, when we get more settled we can have some dinner parties and meet our social responsibilities . . ."

Husband: (interrupting) "That I mocked and shamed you?"

Wife: "You mocked me and shamed me and said, 'Now you are trying to tell me what we are going to do!'"

Husband: "Gee, I don't remember saying anything like that at all. I really don't."

Wife: "You did."

Husband: "Well, I don't remember it at all—not one tiny bit. I can remember talking about dinner parties, but in no way can I remember mocking or shaming or laughing."

Wife: "I don't think that you realize it."

Husband: "If I do, I surely want you to call it to my attention right away."

Wife: (interrupting) "I can't."

Husband: "Why can't you, honey?"

Wife: "I can't say anything; you get mad. I wish we could do like Dr. Fitzgerald once suggested. Find some kind of a signal, even if I have to get a flag. I wish I could find a signal so I wouldn't have to use any words at all."

Husband: (interrupting) But, I don't see why you can't. You already do. When I am angry with Jim, you say 'John.' That's a signal."

Wife: "But I say it softly."

Husband: "Yes, so softly that both kids can hear it, and Jim is twenty feet down the hall."

Wife: "But you sent him away."

Husband: "But I didn't. He had finished dinner, and I said, 'No more arguing. Just go on; keep on going up to your room' . "

Wife: "But you wouldn't listen to him. He was trying to explain something to you and . . ."

Husband: (interrupting) "But I do listen. I don't see how you can tell the difference between when I am listening and when I am not. I heard what he had to say. I don't see how you can say that there are some things I can do and some things I can't do, when you, yourself, do what you wish. Right here sitting in this room you said you would never give anything away, and you have just given away a blackboard. And I resent that."

Wife: "I didn't give it away, I loaned it."

Husband: "It doesn't make any difference whether it is giving or loaning. You did it without consulting me, and it was mine. And you raised the question as to whether a wife can make any decisions on her own. And my answer 234 is, of course, of course, you can, but not when it has to do with something of mine. You had three weeks to think about it, and I see no reason why you couldn't have talked with me about it."

Wife: "Honey, there is no problem now. I have learned. I will never loan or give anything of ours again without talking with you first."

Husband: "Of mine."

Wife: "But, honey, I have tried to explain that in my mind it wasn't yours. The kids were playing with it."

Husband: "That doesn't make sense. If I let Jim use my tennis racket, it's still my tennis racket."

Wife: "We're not getting anywhere with this. I don't see any point in continuing to discuss the question of the blackboard" (pause).

Therapist: (addressing husband) "Were you a debater?"

Husband: "No, why?"

Therapist: "Well, it looks to me, a few minutes ago, like you pulled a very clever debater's trick."

Husband: "What? (Laughs a little.) What was it, I wasn't aware of it?"

Therapist: "Well, Mary was trying to talk with you about some way that she thinks you acted or some way that she felt that you came through—to her, at least. And you abruptly changed the subject back to the blackboard. (And now addressing the wife.) And you went right along with him, just like a trout taking bait."

(In this confrontation and the two that led up to it I address myself to the communicational problem and its purpose as a diversionary ploy on the part of the husband, turning the spotlight back on his wife. I also comment on her part in this interaction.)

Wife: "Yes, I did. I didn't even notice it. I would like to go on to something without your stopping me. I would 235 like you, John, to tell Dr. Fitzgerald just how angry you get with Jim. Do you think it is this much anger or this much (indicating with her hands)?"

Husband: (loudly and stridently) "I don't know, I don't know how to measure it. I was much more angry with you for interfering, but I can't say how much, how angry I was. The whole thing lasted only forty-five seconds, or at the most two minutes. And the whole thing happened a week ago."

Wife: "You were very, very angry."

Husband: "Honey, I couldn't have been that angry. I was still eating dinner, and I finished my dinner. And I don't think I'm half as angry as you get at the kids sometimes, screaming and yelling."

Wife: (addressing Therapist) "It happened like this. John was going to take Jim and Tom to the basketball game. But when I said that I would ride along, and he found out that I was going with them—and this was the fourth week in a row that this happened—John said for us to go ahead without him. Jim asked why it was that every time I decided to go, he decides not to go. I thought that was a sharp question. Tom said, 'I want you to go, we can all go', and you said, 'No, no, if your mother is going I won't.' I know I am not supposed to analyze you, but I am doing it now. It was when Jim asked that question that made you so mad. And then you wouldn't talk with him about it, and he ended up being sent away. And you were so angry. Tom plucked on my sleeve and asked, 'Why is Daddy so angry'."

Husband: "Honey, that's not true. I wasn't that angry, I don't know why you exaggerate these things."

Wife: "You don't realize how angry you get. When I said, 'John,' you leaned across the table, and you pointed your finger at me, and you said, 'You were the cause of all of this and if you don't start getting something out of this therapy we might as well quit because it is costing a lot.

You better start listening.' I'm cringing and the kids are cringing."

Husband: "Honey, oh God. Cringing is so dramatic, I doubt that you cringed. And I do think that we should be getting something out of these sessions, bringing something home, not just having a little game here and then forgetting it when we get home. And you said one time in the car coming here that we would talk here, but nothing would change at home and to me that seemed absurd."

Therapist: (addressing both, but mainly the husband and looking at the husband) "Well, I don't live with you people, and I can't tell how angry either of you were last evening, yesterday, a week ago, or a month ago. And even here I don't have any anger meter that could act with precision. It's a subjective thing, but I think in listening to you I can confirm one thing, John, about your anger. As I listen to you, when Mary is coming through to me as being slightly critical—not really belittling, not really bitter or antagonistic—I can hear the anger in your voice tone and in the number of decibels the volume of your voice increases. And it's seeming to me that you are getting more angry than can be accounted for by the degree of criticism I am hearing. It is almost as if it is hitting some kind of sensitive area in you. I don't know what it is, but it is sounding to me like you are overreacting. It's as if when criticism goes into you, it gets amplified so that it really hurts; and you are reacting as if you had really been stung."

(That Mary seems only slightly critical to me may not be evident without hearing her soft and warm voice tones. Since I am convinced that her criticism is minimal and that her statement represents more an effort to get her husband to look at his anger, I join her in this endeavor. At another opportunity, I shall attempt to get at the wife's sensitivity and fear of small amounts of anger. John agrees in part, but only within the time frame of his marriage.) 237

Husband: "I think you are probably right. And I think I am responding to little incidents that add together, and all of a sudden it builds up very quickly. I think that must happen. I really do, because I think the little incidences, in and of themselves, are not that important, but they build up. I must augment one little incident with all of those that have gone before. And all of a sudden I get the full impact of all of them added together. It's something that has built up over ten years. Of all those times, when I was angry at Jim and was criticized for it."

Therapist: "By the way, are you liking yourself when you are angry with Jim or afterwards?"

(Since I suspect an unconscious identification with his hated and feared father, I approach this gingerly. It would be tactless to confront him directly with his likeness to his father.)

Husband: "No, not at all. And as a matter of fact, I don't think there is a time that I haven't thought about it afterwards and—if I thought that there was any possibility that I had overreacted—and I didn't go back to him and talk with him about it, and apologize. And that can happen with either Jim or Tom; and I usually do it privately. I can remember an incident back a couple of weeks ago when Mary wasn't even home. I was babysitting, and the kids were messing around about going to bed. And I thought that I got too angered and I should not have. And I apologized to both of them directly later on. I told them that I was sorry. I am aware of this and always apologize."

Therapist: "Okay, I think we have got something here concerning your anger. When you get mad with either of the kids, you are not liking yourself either immediately or subsequently. You are coming down pretty hard on yourself. You are already operating under a lot of inner self-criticism, and, when Mary comes along and adds a straw or a couple

238

of ounces to what's already there, it becomes almost more than you can bear."

(In this interpretation I explain what I believe to be the intrapsychic and interpersonal dynamics operating in the here-and-now, without touching the genetic material. In my subsequent comment, interrupting the wife and blocking her out, I press forward with my exploration, seeking the husband's cooperation in the search.)

Husband: "Well, I really know that I get angry at her when she interferes."

Therapist: "But I am wondering if it is really the interference so much as it is your experiencing the interference as disapproval or criticism."

Husband: "Disapproval of me?"

Therapist: "Yeah."

Wife: "Well, it has been hard for me. You may not know it—and apparently you don't—but for every time I interfere there are a hundred times that I remain silent and don't. Really, I do have some discipline."

Therapist: (interrupting) "Before we go on, I need to clarify something. It is not clear to me, John, whether you had any evidence within yourself that I might be accurate about the disapproval thing—that my hypothesis about what happens might be accurate—that you react like you have really been attacked, seriously attacked."

Husband: "Well, I don't know for sure. I have thought about it as being a sort of straw-that-broke-the-camel's-back kind of thing. I have thought about it that way. Because I have really thought a number of times that I am really tired of all the little things that cause arguments. And I feel that I have just got to draw the line somewhere. I am just not going to take any more interference in certain situations—none whatsoever. Each little incident in itself is insignificant or almost insignificant, not totally. And then I think 239 that I don't have to put up with this anymore—this has to stop and stop abruptly. So I must feel in myself that, by God, I have drawn a line, and I am really angry."

Wife: "But haven't you said that same thing many years ago, not just recently. I can hear you saying those exact same words just after Tom was born."

Husband: "I don't remember."

Wife: "Well, that's what I remember. It was about that time that you said exactly those same words to me. I have been bending to you, and I am not going to do it any-more—words like that."

Husband: "I don't know. I may have. And if I did, I am sure that I felt that way at the time. But let me say right now, I have been criticized for bringing up things that happened in the past. And right now I hear you saying, 'Didn't you say those same words a number of years ago.' It seems to be all right for you to drag up the past, but not for me to do so, as far as you are concerned. I think I resent criticism of me when I see that very same fault in you. I see you sometimes as careless, and I resent it when you say to me, 'You've got to be careful.' And it bothers me when you interfere with what I do with the kids, when I make it a point to not interfere with you. I get up and leave the room and close the door so I won't hear it."

Wife: "How often?"

Husband: "Almost all of the time, if not all the time."

Therapist: "As a matter of fact, Mary, just a couple of minutes ago I felt like giving you a karate chop in the liver. I was trying to get John to take a look at something that might be going on within himself and then you came long and messed it up."

(This is a very confronting remark. It reflects exactly how I felt at the moment. If I am to attain my goal with the husband, it 240 is important to prevent interference by the wife.)

Wife: "Isn't it important that he said that same thing years ago?"

Therapist: "Well, it seems to me like rubbing his nose in it. (Pause. Therapist continues.) Now, I am not in any way saying that that is what you intended to do, but we react to others on the basis of how they are coming through, not what they might be intending deep inside" (pause).

(I follow up with another confrontation. When I perceive the wife's hurt feelings in her nonverbal reaction and the long pause, I make a gentle interpretation and give her credit for good intentions, whether they are actually there or not.)

Wife: "Now I am feeling embarrassed. I was thinking that time was important, and I didn't mean to put him down. I was thinking of the time element. But here I am justifying myself again (pause). But he didn't give me a karate chop; he only felt like it."

Therapist: (humorously) "Saying it is good insurance against doing it. If we don't say things promptly enough, and they build up, then it might even build up to the level of doing it or getting close to it. (Pause. Therapist looking at husband.) What are you thinking about over there? You seem pensive."

(On one occasion the husband did slap his wife. I emphasize therefore the value of verbal aggression. Then I return to the husband to continue where we left off.)

Husband: "I was just trying to think where we were in the interaction before we got to the time thing."

Therapist: "We were trying to explore your sensitivity to criticism. We were trying to understand it—make some sense of it."

Husband: "Okay, I recognize sensitivity in some areas. 241

For example, because I am the father and because we have two sons, I think the question of role modeling is important for them. And I think for a long time it was clear that the head of the family was not me. And it may have been that at first I didn't want to and it could just be me. In a marriage it takes two people to set things up, and it seems to me—and I am not talking about my anger here—that in certain ways it is important for boys to identify with their fathers in the same way that it is important for girls to identify with their mothers. I think that it is healthy. Now in Mary's family, I think that it was very fortunate that there were no boys. I feel that you grew up in a family where the mother was very strong and your father was very weak. And that would not have been good for a boy. And sometimes I don't think that you are aware of what a model for a father might be or should be."

Wife: "Are you relating this to your activities in our home, your place in our family? You are athletic; you participate with the boys in sports."

Husband: "No, not just that—everything I have to do with the boys, how I look to them, the whole bit."

Wife: "There is no doubt in any of our minds that you are the leader of the family."

Husband: "Well, there is in mine."

Wife: "There isn't in mine. Mother may make some decisions, but . . ."

Husband: (interrupting) "Wait, there is in mine."

Wife: "But there shouldn't be."

Husband: "Well, there is. Especially when I can't get mad at anyone without being reprimanded by you. But you can get angry with anyone, and you don't get reprimanded by me. When you are in an argument with our Tom or Jim, I think that it would be irresponsible for me to walk in and say, 'What's going on here?'"

242   Therapist: "Let's take a look at something before we get

too far from it. Your use of the word reprimand suggests the possibility that you are feeling like you are doing something bad."

(My inference is that husband is feeling like a bad child vis-à-vis his wife and his superego. In my next question I invite the husband to find the source of his own sense of badness and praise him when he succeeds.)

Husband: "I do think I am bad when I get angry."

Therapist: "Ah, okay. Now, could you follow the trail of the notion of role model which you mentioned and ask yourself why you might dislike yourself or feel that you are bad when you are angry?"

Husband: "Yeah. Do you want to know the first thing that came to mind? My dad when he was angry."

Therapist: "Yeah."

Husband: "Right off the bat."

Therapist: "Very good."

Wife: "Yes, and we talked about that."

Husband: "But I don't think he ever had the misgiving after he was angry as I do. I don't ever remember being apologized to, and I don't think that any of my brothers or sisters were. But I almost always know if I have been too angry, and I make it up in a few minutes, a half hour, or an hour later without any help—without any help at all from anyone. And I don't think I have ever been so angry that I have been vicious or anything like."

Therapist: "How could Mary help with your feelings (pause)? Do you know any way you could help him, Mary?"

(This is an irrelevant question. He has already made it abundantly clear that he needs to be left alone.)

Wife: "I don't know how I could help. I try to be under- 243 standing, and it comes out analyzing. And I try to be reasonable, and it comes out lecturing."

Husband: "How about not saying anything at all. I don't really need any help. I get angry when you interfere, so it would be better if you would just say nothing."

Wife: "I have tried that, and change just doesn't come. And I want change."

Husband: "Change doesn't come?"

Wife: "There are good days and bad days, but overall change hasn't come."

Husband: "Do you think that I get overly angry with the kids?"

Wife: "Yes, I do."

Husband: "Well, I don't think so. It seems to me that I have been the main disciplinarian of both, especially of Jim. And most of the time you made all kinds of excuses for his behavior. Now, it seems to me that his rapport is better with me than it is with you. I can really talk with Jim about a lot of things, not that I approve of everything he does."

Wife: "And who hollers at me if I say anything at all and Jim rebels against your rules? If he thought that they were so fair, why would he rebel so much? He gets pretty angry."

Husband: "Yes, his first reaction is very aggressive, very aggressive towards me. But later on, he settles down and obeys. His first response is to shout and try to bully you into changing your mind, but I know that ten or fifteen minutes later we can be talking quietly."

Wife: "Then he sees the same thing in us. You can be terribly angry with me, we can have a terrible argument, but it doesn't last long. And after a while we are again talking quietly and reasonably."

Husband: "But I don't think I bully you at all, not at all. On a scale of zero to a hundred, I think I must be at the second or third percentile."

Therapist: "Let's go back to something that I consider important. Mary, it seems to me that I heard John making it very clear that he feels he doesn't need any help at all with his anger—that left to his own devices, he would be able to think it over, calm down, apologize to the kids, if necessary, and makes his peace with them. And I am wondering whether your being upset about his anger has ever permitted you to really give waiting and being quiet a fair-enough trial. It seems to me that I have observed that kind of thing here during our sessions. When he becomes angry, you become very tense, maybe scared. And that leads you to say something intended to calm him down, which in point of fact makes matters worse."

Wife: "Well, it seems to me that I have given it a good trial. I don't know whether John even noticed it, but about two years ago I made up my mind to say nothing. And I think I succeeded for about three or four weeks. I would busy myself in the basement or go out in the garden, so that I think then I did give it a trial, and it didn't work."

Therapist: "Well, now that we are in a therapy situation, how about giving it a trial again?"

(Here I wish to avoid a discussion of the past and encourage the wife to respect her mate's wishes in the present. By implication I am challenging the husband to modify his temper outbursts. If this works, the payoff may be enough to result in the complimentary changes becoming relatively enduring.)

Wife: "For how long."
Therapist: "How about a week until our next session."
Wife: "That seems reasonable. I'll give it a try."
Therapist: "Okay. Now I have one more thing to say—or rather a question to raise with John. Psychologically, as a kind of rule of the thumb, if we react or overreact automati- 245

cally to someone else's behavior, where does that come
from?"

*(In this leading question I wish to help the husband carry his
role-model concept one step further and also to enhance the wife's
understanding of him.)*

Husband: "The unconscious."
Therapist: "Yeah, but what's in there?"
Husband: "Everything."
Therapist: "Well, I guess I am being a little obtuse. I will
come directly to my point. If we react automatically—zap—to
a kid when he is acting up some way, the chances are very
very good that our reaction reflects the way we were treated
under similar circumstances when we were kids. So that
you become your parents of the past and the child becomes
you, so that there is some merit in the notion that we are
reared by our grandparents."

*(Since he can't get there on his own, I have to make my interpretation
directly.)*

Husband: "That makes sense. I will have to think about
that and watch myself."
Wife: "I have some thoughts about that, but I think that
it would be better for me to keep quiet about them."
Therapist: "Right, it sounds like a very good idea." (Husband and wife both laugh.)"

*(The wife is already putting my suggestion into practice, and I
wish to support her in this. The laughter is prognostically encouraging.)*

Therapist: "Our time is up for now. We will meet next
week at the same time."

Index